THE DIVERSITY RECRUITING BLUEPRINT

Your Guide To Crafting An Impactful Inclusion Hiring Strategy

CODY L HORTON

Cody L. Horton, Publisher
Amazon Edition

Cody L. Horton
1801 Red Bud Lane, Suite B-202
Round Rock, TX 78664
Email: cody@codylhorton.com
LinkedIn: https://www.linkedin.com/in/diversityrecruiter/

CONTENTS

PART IV: STEERING AND FRAMEWORK

ACKNOWLEDGMENTS

Special thanks go to Jonathan Kidder, a/k/a the "WizardSourcer," for his encouragement in writing this book. He's a top-notch technical recruiter, published author, and creator of the blog WizardSourcer, a well-known source of recruiting knowledge that has helped countless sourcers and recruiters since 2015. Thanks, Jonathan, for your generosity, encouragement, and thoughtful input throughout this process.

I owe a huge Thank You to Torin Ellis, diversity strategist, published author, and SiriusXM contributor, for his guidance and commitment to being a DEI pioneer.

You are always a source of inspiration; without your many contributions to DEI, this book would have been released before it should have been. Thanks, Torin, for your feedback and insight.

I owe Chris Bell and Simon Mullins a round of applause for their insight on Leadership and Executive Recruiting. Simon and Chris shared a wealth of knowledge on strategic talent acquisition and executive search to help me highlight critical topics related to executive hiring.

If you've picked up this book, you (or your company) may be struggling with building a *diverse and inclusive organization.* Or perhaps, you are curious and want to determine if there's a better way to do what you've already been doing.

It's my hope that, after reading this book, you will be able to:

- Achieve success with your diversity and inclusion hiring and growth.

- <u>Understand</u> key terms associated with diversity, inclusion, equity, and belonging.
- <u>Discuss</u> what diversity means and how it impacts talent pipelines.
- <u>Identify</u> and <u>mitigate</u> bias in the hiring process.
- <u>Create</u> frameworks to support diversity recruiting efforts.
- <u>Identify</u> and <u>expand</u> diverse organizations and resources.
- <u>Discuss</u> and <u>demonstrate</u> knowledge of diversity sourcing techniques.
- <u>Leverage</u> tools to ensure inclusive messaging in recruiting content.
- <u>Gain insight</u> into coaching and consulting with stakeholders on DEI hiring efforts.
- <u>Identify</u> data sources to help with diversity hiring plans.

I want to share how you can measure success in your diversity and inclusion efforts. I also want you to be able to interact with the content in this book which will allow you to build a strategy as you go through the book.

But first, let's define what it is that I'm talking about when I refer to *diversity, inclusion, and equity.*

Diversity refers to the range of characteristics that distinguish each of us. Our diversity is shaped by our histories, personalities, experiences, and beliefs, which form our views of the world, our perspectives, and our methods of interacting with our environment.

Inclusion happens when people feel respected and valued for their contribution to the workforce, and by extension, society, regardless of their circumstances or personal traits. Inclusion happens when people have:

- *access to opportunities and resources*
- *the ability to give their personal best in every interaction*
- *the ability to contribute their ideas and talents to enhance their organization*
- *the ability to bring considerably more of themselves to their professions*
- *the feeling that they belong*

E quity is created by intentionally, purposefully, and consciously ensuring that everyone in the organization has access to the help, resources, treatment, and opportunities needed to succeed at work.

WHY I KEEP GOING

Why did I start this business and write this book?

The answer is simple yet complex. I wanted to discuss my vision to empower people to change their lives and my mission to connect great people to great opportunities. My goal is to create systemic change in the talent acquisition world that outlives my life and our company.

More importantly, I need to share what keeps me going. Why do I keep going, and what is the motivation behind my continuous work on Diversity and Inclusion recruiting? I desire to share the things that I've experienced early in my life, such as being teased and being a very sensitive kid who was told, "You need to develop thicker skin and stop being so *sensitive*," and things like not being invited to sleepovers with my white friends.

Things like being criticized and sometimes even threatened by the fathers of my white girlfriends. The experiences of being taunted for my lips, color, size, and weight. The quiet realization of being ignored by peers in meetings and not being heard. The exclusion surrounding bits and pieces of my journey does not have to be everyone else's reality.

These experiences are the things that drive me to keep going. I stay focused and use that as my motivation and fuel to keep doing this work as I progress through the adversity of being a leader and entrepreneur with a mission, vision, and calling to empower people to change their lives.

This book will help others find a way to assist other people who have been marginalized in the job market, and I know that the topics in this book will move us closer to becoming more inclusive with our recruiting efforts.

I thank my wife, Dorothy, and my daughters, Chelsea and Ashley, for their support on this journey.

PART I

DIVERSITY

"It is not our differences that divide us. It is our inability to
recognize, accept, and celebrate those differences."
~ Audre Lorde

GLOBAL DIVERSITY TREE

My good friend, and inspirational ID&E speaker and consultant, Eddie Pate, has created what he calls a Global Diversity Tree. This tool is an insightful way to discuss the topic of diversity, equity, and inclusion, and in my opinion, it's something that every organization should use as a part of its diversity hiring efforts.

When you share this tool with your team, tell them that the tree represents one possible combination of visible and invisible dimensions; however, it's in no way an exhaustive list of what makes individuals diverse.

Instead, it represents a visual illustration of how companies conceptualize and characterize diversity. Essentially, what you see above ground are "visible" and known dimensions of diversity.

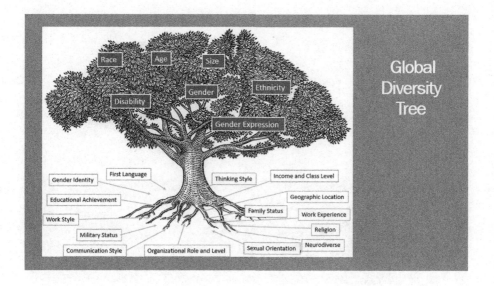

The dimensions below ground are often those diversity dimensions that are less known or are invisible unless you have specific knowledge about a particular person.

There isn't a particular strength associated with an above-ground versus below-ground dimension. Dimensions vary in importance depending on the person and how they self-identify. In other words, race may trigger a stronger sense of identity in one person relative to another.

Another person may place more importance on culture or ethnicity to define who they are or how they act. There isn't one perfect tree and, in fact, what gets listed above ground or below ground will vary depending on geographic location, perspective, and experiences.

The bottom line is this, the lesson to learn is that there is no single correct diversity tree, i.e., the tree can vary by geography, and it needs to be contextual with where you are.

This is the beauty of it.

Eddie Pate
Founder and Chief ID&E Officer
Eddie Pate Speaking and Consulting, Inc.
eddiepate21@gmail.com /206 948-0900

Website: http://eddiepate-speaking.com/
LinkedIn: https://www.linkedin.com/

INCLUSION INSPIRES INNOVATION

CHAPTER ONE

WHY DIVERSITY AND INCLUSION

In order to excel in today's marketplace, businesses must consider diversity and inclusion. Diversity is the variety of characteristics that make up a population, and inclusion is the process of making everyone feel included in the workplace. The benefits of diversity and inclusion are numerous. It allows for creativity and innovation to flourish while consistently improving the company's ability to make better decisions.

Additionally, a diverse and inclusive workforce leads to improved morale, decreased employee turnover, and increased productivity.

What is an Inclusive Workplace?

When we talk about the importance of an inclusive workplace, what we're really talking about is the importance of creating an environment at work where everyone feels like they belong, regardless of their background or identity. This sense of belonging is key to employee productivity and engagement.

Inclusive workplaces are also more effective because they don't rely on tokenism. Tokenism is when a company hires a few people from marginalized groups to give the appearance of being diverse, but they don't put the resources, systems, and support structures in place to support authentic inclusion at scale. This can have the opposite effect of what's intended because it can make people feel like they're not valued for their skills and talents, but rather for their identity.

An inclusive workplace is one that celebrates diversity, equity, and inclusion. It's a place where everyone feels welcome and appreciated, and where everyone has an opportunity to succeed. It looks and feels like a level playing field and isn't just a performative check in the box.

What Is a Diversified Workplace?

A diversified workplace is an environment where individuals from different religious backgrounds, cultures, sexual orientations, and educational backgrounds are able to come together and work cooperatively.

This type of environment is beneficial for both the employees and the company as a whole because it allows for different perspectives to be shared and diversity to be embraced. Additionally, a diversified workplace is one that is inclusive and provides equity for all employees. This type of environment allows employees to feel like they belong and are part of a larger community. *What is the difference between diversity, inclusion, and belonging?*

People often use the words "diversity, inclusion, and belonging" interchangeably, but there is a big difference between these terms.

- Diversity is having a variety of people in a group or organization.
- Inclusion is making everyone feel welcome and equal.
- Belonging means feeling safe and accepted in a group or organization.

Creating an inclusive environment means that everyone feels like they can contribute to the group and that their contributions are valued equally. It also means that everyone feels safe and comfortable in the group. A sense of belonging allows people to be themselves without fear of judgment or exclusion.

Organizations that focus on diversity alone often have a token member or two from underrepresented groups, but they don't always feel welcome or included. Whereas organizations that focus on inclusion ensure everyone feels welcome and can participate fully. A workplace that celebrates diversity, but does not value inclusion will not be successful. Underrepresented individuals will feel like outsiders, and will not be able to contribute to their full potential.

On the other hand, a workplace that values inclusion but does not have a diverse workforce will also be unsuccessful. The differences in perspectives and experiences of the employees will not be brought to the table, and the company will miss out on valuable ideas. Creating a culture of diversity and inclusion is essential for any organization looking to thrive in today's global economy.

Why is Diversity and Inclusion in the workplace important?

There is a strong business case for diversity and inclusion in the workplace. A report by McKinsey & Company found that companies in the top quartile for racial and ethnic diversity are 35 percent more likely to have above-average profitability than those in the bottom quartile. And companies in the top quartile for gender diversity are 15 percent more likely to have above-average profitability.

Diversity and inclusion also lead to increased innovation and creativity. Teams with a diversity of thought are better able to problem-solve and come up with new ideas. In fact, studies show that diverse teams are up to 45 percent more innovative than homogeneous teams.

A lack of diversity can also lead to employee attrition. Employees want to feel like they belong somewhere, and when they don't see themselves represented in their workplace, they may choose to leave.

The Advantages of having a Diverse Workplace

Innovation and creativity.
A diverse workplace is a key ingredient for creativity and innovation. Diverse teams are more likely to come up with new ideas because they have a variety of perspectives to draw from.

Increased productivity.
A diverse workplace also leads to increased productivity. When everyone comes from different backgrounds, they are more likely to approach tasks in different ways. This can lead to greater efficiency and faster problem-solving.

Better retention.
A diverse workplace also helps with employee retention and employer branding. Employees want to work for companies that embrace diversity, and customers want to do business with companies that reflect their values. Therefore, a diverse workplace is good for business!

Expanded market.
You need a diversified workforce if you want to market to a variety of consumers. When you hire people from various backgrounds, languages, experiences, etc., you can ensure that your business will appeal to a larger target market. In addition, your employees will be able to relate to customers from all walks of life since they themselves come from diverse backgrounds.

Increased revenue.
Any business must prioritize growing its revenue. Your ultimate objective of increasing earnings will be closer to reality if you make full use of a diverse staff. According to a recent Boston Consulting Group study, businesses with a diverse staff and more innovative practices made 19 percent more revenue than those with lower diversity scores. The stats prove it.

The Challenges of a Diverse Workforce

Unfair prejudices.

Unfortunately, some people are intolerant of those who are different from them. Racial, sexual, or even religious discrimination may come from this.

If these issues arise within your organization, they may result in an unsettling (and potentially dangerous) work environment and harm the standing of your business. Therefore, you must put into place consistent approaches and policies to address and prevent any form of discrimination or harassment at work and take corrective or disciplinary action.

Communication issues.

A diverse team will include people who speak different languages, have different backgrounds, and live in different locations. Employee communication may suffer as a result of these differences, which will have a detrimental effect on how productive your business will be.

It is essential to ensure that organizations with multilingual employees establish ways to increase communication among their team members. Establishing culture discussions, site visits, and providing tools and processes that help team members connect and learn about different cultures is critical.

For example, rather than relying on automatic translation tools, have native speakers review content to ensure that the translation is correct in meaning and context for the intended recipients. Keep the intended audience in mind and work with your global team to check the nuance of the message and the communications channel(s) that may be best to use.

Words and context matter.

For your global workforce you can improve your success by getting assistance from organizations and tools like GlobeSmart, Hofstede Insights, Cultural Navigator and Global Business Culture. These and other platforms give you information on global cultures and provide you with foundational first steps to establishing a more culturally aware approach to creating an inclusive workplace.

There are a variety of culture and translation tools on the market to help improve your communication with a diverse workforce. For example, sending employees to language-learning sessions, and sharing global team history, culture, foods, and stories about life in different countries is another way to move your global communication forward. Your company will expand, and more success opportunities will become available if you can close the communication gap between employees.

Cultural differences regarding professional etiquette.

Different cultures have their own, distinctive traditions. This includes their attitudes toward and their manners on the job, which as a result, could lead to miscommunications and even hostility between team members.

Leaders should be mindful of creating processes at the headquarters and rolling them out to their geographically diverse workforce without first soliciting input from employees and regions not based at the headquarters.

Products, services, and policies often fail because they were created at the central HQ and pushed out to the global or regional employees to localize before there was an opportunity for the broader workforce to highlight potential issues unique to their location and population.

Take the time needed to get input from the communities within your company that may experience new policies differently, and it will increase trust and adoption more quickly than having to redo after a hastily implemented initiative.

Think globally and act locally.

Make sure your staff takes the time to consider, invest, and respect one another's customs, concerns, and cultures to overcome miscommunication and avoid unnecessary conflicts.

How Do You Recruit Diverse Candidates?

You must change your recruitment strategies if you desire to draw diverse candidates to your hiring process. Here are some ideas you might want to keep in mind:

☐ Expand your talent pool to include people with different backgrounds.
☐ Highlight your commitment to diversity.
☐ Use job boards that serve diverse candidates.
☐ Be careful to include a diverse group of people when choosing your interview panel.

Although you can find different individuals on your own by using a variety of channels, it might be a better use of your resources to engage in sourcing support for your recruitment needs.

CHAPTER TWO

OVERALL TA FRAMEWORK

Before I dive deep into how diversity, equity, inclusion, and belonging should be approached from a talent acquisition, assessment, and retention perspective, it's essential to understand what makes that approach effective—the framework.

Since I have a talent acquisition leader, or talent management leader, viewpoint, I see through a talent perspective how vital a framework is to an organization's success. A framework is multilayered. It's a guide, a context, and an environment; it's the toolkit that shapes everything from approach and perspective to outcomes.

If we think of sports, the framework would be:

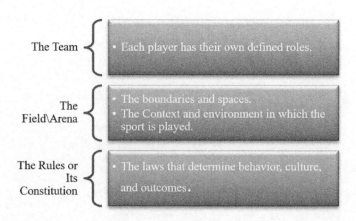

The Team
- Each player has their own defined roles.

The Field\Arena
- The boundaries and spaces.
- The Context and environment in which the sport is played.

The Rules or Its Constitution
- The laws that determine behavior, culture, and outcomes.

And what drives everything, and the piece we often forget, is the purpose.

Why are we even playing this game?

Your talent acquisition organization's whole purpose is to enable your business to accomplish its goals and support the customers. Talent acquisition is in place and exists for the sole purpose of ensuring that your business can reach its revenue, product, and service goals by having the right people in the right seats. To get the right people in those seats, we must have a clear strategy, perspective, and approach.

For the talent acquisition (TA) leader, it's essential to ensure they are looking at an enterprise-wide approach and engagement. The enterprise might be a global enterprise if you're a multinational organization. It may be a national strategy, or it may be a regional strategy. If you're just one location, one office, then it's the strategy that encompasses that whole location and all the people who are going to be players and who are going to contribute to the talent acquisition strategy. For the TA leader, or talent manager leaders, to execute a game-winning strategy, they must be organized. As a result, several big buckets require the TA leader's attention.

Recruiter And Their Recruiting Capability

There is the bucket of the recruiter and their recruiting capability. This is what allows you to go out and find passive candidates, engage active candidates, and get out and get the talent to engage with you and participate in your efforts.

Engagement And Onboarding

The next big bucket is on how you attract people and, once you attract them, how you assess them in your interview process to get them hired. More importantly, once they are hired, you must evaluate if you completed the hire with effective onboarding. For example, is there a thirty, sixty, or ninety-day plan for onboarding?

Employment Brand

Then, there's the employment brand. What is the message that candidates are going to get when they think about your brand? Do you have an inclusive brand? Do you have a brand that resonates with people? Are you working with your marketing and PR organization to ensure that the content reflects and represents your organization?

Your marketing is a message to potential candidates. What that message represents and communicates is critical because one of the first things they're going to do is look at your employment brand to see if they know you, if they like you, and if they're going to trust you.

Consultant And Trusted Advisor?

The next bucket is for the recruiters and your talent acquisition professionals. Whether it's a recruiter, a sourcer, or a coordinator, you want to make sure they are advisors and consultants that the hiring managers in your interview team trust. They must be willing to take guidance and direction from them because they understand the value your team brings to the table.

Some of the framework and perspective-setting of your strategy will be ensuring your recruiting teams aren't just focused on recruiting and hiring, but they understand the context of the business and what the business is trying to do. That's why being a trusted advisor is so critical. Your recruiters need to be able to coach and consult the hiring and interview teams.

Importance Of Data

How do you determine success when your team has a clear goal and vision, and the strategy has been executed? Success has to be measured, so along with a clear plan, there must be a data-driven approach. This last key component will determine the longevity and overall organizational success.

Decisions must be based on data, but you must also understand what data is necessary and what you're looking for and measuring. Above all, you must be able to interpret the data and understand what that data is telling you.

The story around the data is what you'll share with the leadership team, whether it's the CEO or other board members. From there, you'll be in the optimal position to take action based on the data and make well-informed judgments and adjustments. Data will underscore everything we discussed and allow you to know where you are at all times in every step of your strategy.

So as the head of talent acquisition, you always want to be able to look through the enterprise lens when constructing your framework for talent acquisition.

Additionally, always keep these critical contributing factors in mind:

- Recruiter capability
- How do you attract, assess, hire, and onboard new hires?
- Employment brand
- Being a trusted advisor
- Making data-driven, business-influenced decisions.

All of this facilitates the overarching framework, and everything under diversity and inclusion would be tangential while still touching on this part of the business and the recruiting process.

Now, let's get into diversity.

PART II

COMMUNICATING THROUGH DIVERSITY

"Strength lies in differences, not in similarities."
~ Stephen Covey.

CHAPTER THREE

BEST IN CLASS HIGHLIGHTS

For best results, people should understand the key terms associated with diversity, equity, inclusion, and belonging. They should be able to discuss what each term means and how it impacts their business. They should also be comfortable identifying and mitigating bias in the hiring process.

Terminology and concepts I'll discuss in this chapter include:

- ☐ Diverse leadership
- ☐ Transparency
- ☐ Authentic messages
- ☐ Measuring results

I'll also share how to:

- Break down silos
- Take risks
- Lead from the front
- Embrace change
- Evaluate transferrable skills
- Develop your inclusion statement

Some of the best-in-class organizations are making great progress in terms of diversity and inclusion in their workforce and offer a great role model for any company that wants to be successful with its diversity, equity, and inclusion (DEI) efforts.

These organizations are clear in their understanding of what diversity, inclusion, equity, and belonging involve, and they're clear on their company goals for diversity. They know what they need to do to reach their goals and are working towards them.

People see what they've seen in the past, and sometimes they're not open to seeing what a person could be. But a best-in-class organization will see the inclusive and diverse workforce that they want to build, starting with the end in mind. If you start with the end in mind, you will get to the ultimate goal.

Let's consider an example of the Broadway play and movie production analogy.

> When a director is planning a movie and or a production on Broadway, they all know what the end result is going to be, and they know the purpose.
>
> If those were the only issues, it would be amazing and easy, but they must also solve the challenges associated with recruiting and casting the right performers for each role.
>
> They have to work through finding the right props and costumes, adhere to production schedules, and meet timelines to deliver on the announced release dates and locations.
>
> They have to work with their teams to find and assign understudies and backup performers, including all cast members, extras, and production crew members, to ensure that the production is a success and ends with a successful launch, favorable reviews, and applause from the audience.

There are many unseen challenges beneath the surface that the audience doesn't think about or recognize.

Each cast and crew member faces invisible challenges that they must work through, which include:

- investing many hours learning their lines
- getting into character by studying the characters in the story
- bringing the character to life for the audience

Oftentimes, performers face confidence issues and imposter syndrome or misalignment with the playwright's vision of the character.

Filming and special effects teams are challenged with physical locations, accessibility, safety, lighting, and other environmental issues that impact the quality of the production.

There is no cookie-cutter solution to a successful production, and every team member must play their role and collaborate with a diverse cast and crew to achieve the result of a standing ovation during and at the end of the performance.

When the production is at risk of not meeting the release day, the producer and director must work together to prioritize what gets cut or changed to meet the release date, or they may decide to push the release date further in the future. This decision is not made in a vacuum and involves many people, advertisers, theaters, and social and economic factors which persuade and eventually influence the decision.

Workplace DEI efforts are similar. This work cannot be done in a vacuum and depends on many inputs. It can be overwhelming if you attempt to solve all of your DEI efforts alone.

The key is to work with others, align your efforts, ask for help, and, most importantly, get all the players to visualize the workforce and workplace that they want to see. Work with all the players to create the inclusive company that you desire the most.

HR is in a pivotal position to work with leaders to guide the journey and help the organization move forward.

Now, you need all the players:

- ☐ Senior Leaders
- ☐ Hiring Managers
- ☐ Employees
- ☐ Recruiters

You need all those people to be involved, but the senior leaders must lead and be in front, leading the organization's commitment to your inclusion and diversity efforts.

Senior leaders are in the best position to provide resources, budget, and commitment to the overall framework and strategy. They have the broadest reach and can use that reach to motivate and inspire people, and they also have the ability to assign resources to individuals and teams to ensure that goals are met. HR plays a critical role in keeping the right people moving forward and coaching other members, but your diversity and inclusion efforts must have senior leader engagement and influence.

As a result, your DEI Leader should:

- ✓ Play a key role in helping leaders communicate the vision and provide coaching and guidance to ensure leaders continue to lead when they get tired or face competing obstacles that impact the goal of creating a diverse and inclusive workplace.
- ✓ Be instrumental in helping the organization appropriately establish data-driven analysis and metrics to measure progress along the DEI journey.
- ✓ Not be the savior of the organization and should not be expected to solve the organization's issues alone, but they will be able to hold up the mirror for the organization to see itself through a lens that leaders may not be willing to look through.
- ✓ Be a partner to all cross-company leaders and functions. The best thing that you can do is give your DEI leader the budget, resources,

and authority to drive change, consult external professionals, and hold leaders and managers accountable for moving the needle forward on cultural and systemic changes.

✓ Be a partner in operationalizing your Diversity Recruiting Strategy.

Breaking Down Silos

Silos exist in most of our enterprises, large or small, regardless of size. And it's these silos that may impede the advancement of change. As a leader, breaking down silos is one action you can take to further your efforts in diversity, inclusion, equity, and belonging.

For instance, one simple example of a silo is the one that might exist between HR and the recruiting team. It is easy for HR and Recruiting to become sileod and focused only on their part of the work. The silo is broken down and reduced when there is better communication and the focus on a common goal. Since HR and Recruiting teams tend to report to the Chief People Officer, there is a good chance that there will be good alignment with goals and frequent communication. When you consider the entire firm or other divisions like supply chain, engineering, and some many others, you'll discover that communication isn't always effective and goals are not always aligned.

Additionally, when we are concentrating on people, we want to ensure company-wide sharing of best practices. You're in a terrific position as a hiring manager to communicate with your colleagues across the entire company. If you work for a small business, it might not be difficult to do this because you can simply walk over to the next employee or pick up the phone.

In a large organization, it may be more complicated to reach the right stakeholders or peers because of the organization's size, geographic locations around the world, or overall organizational structure. Getting alignment may require a more sophisticated approach to communicating across a globally matrixed organization than it would require for a smaller organization. It may require working through the organizational chart to find a peer or responsible party. So sharing best practices and gaining alignment may take longer, but don't let that stop you.

These are some of the action items that you'd want to focus on in order to get those silos broken down as a hiring manager because you have influence, and you have peers. The next page will show you a few key steps to remove silos.

5 Key Steps of Removing
Silos

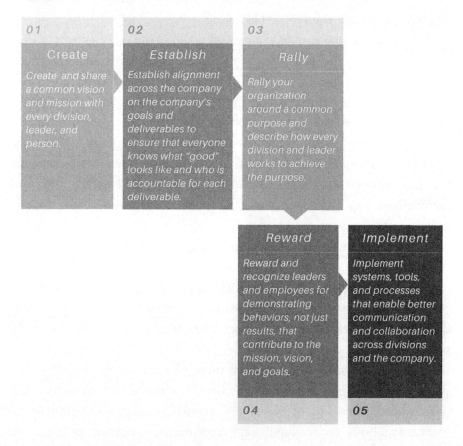

01 **Create**
Create and share a common vision and mission with every division, leader, and person.

02 **Establish**
Establish alignment across the company on the company's goals and deliverables to ensure that everyone knows what "good" looks like and who is accountable for each deliverable.

03 **Rally**
Rally your organization around a common purpose and describe how every division and leader works to achieve the purpose.

04 **Reward**
Reward and recognize leaders and employees for demonstrating behaviors, not just results, that contribute to the mission, vision, and goals.

05 **Implement**
Implement systems, tools, and processes that enable better communication and collaboration across divisions and the company.

Embracing Change

Without a standard of what constitutes DEI, every organization is left to determine what that looks like. Hence, businesses are beginning to understand that if they want to integrate diversity into their cultures, they must also make equity and inclusion part of their efforts.

Diversity, equity, inclusion, and belonging have ramifications that go far beyond ensuring varied representation in a community. A DEI framework requires company-wide acceptance in addition to tracking diversity metrics.

DEI data

Data from your diversity efforts needs to be clearly presented and understood by everyone in the organization. Not all data is equal; information must be understood by the target audience in order to be actionable and have a chance to change behavior.

In other words, people reviewing the data need to know exactly how it will impact the organization, both culturally and financially. This is especially true with leadership, as the financial health of the organization is one of its top priorities.

When these individuals see the myriad benefits of diversity, they will not only be in agreement with your DEI efforts, but they will actively support them, and will be willing to take on risks they might not otherwise have done.

Leadership

Senior leaders must be engaged and lead from the front.

What I mean is that business leaders have to set the tone for DEI and ensure that others see them championing and modeling behaviors that promote inclusion and belonging. Leaders set the tone, and the employees will follow the leader.

For example: When a controversial issue arises, leaders need to lean in and show employees that they are not just sticking their heads in the sand and hoping the problem will go away.

True DEI leaders take a stand and provide the resources and air cover for their teams to tackle the challenge. Over the past few years, we have seen an increasing number of social justice issues arise. From the killing of unarmed citizens to mass shootings, we can count on a few fingers the number of corporate leaders who have taken a stand against those issues.

As it relates to hiring, some leaders acknowledge that they need more representation of women and underrepresented people, but few are willing to take a stand and demand that their teams get past the bias of hiring the same profile for top executive roles. Leading from the front means looking at what the C-suite looks like and taking steps to identify women and diverse talent to fill roles at that level.

One of my former companies recognized the need for more women and underrepresented populations on the executive team. However, when it came time to hire, the leader failed to take a stand and chose to allow other executives to screen out talent because their diverse slate of candidates was not a "culture fit" and didn't fit in the existing leadership team's background, education, and years of experience.

Leading from the front means the senior executive would require others to check their bias and decide whether an executive on the team needed to have all of the nice-to-have qualifications that the company had historically hired for a C-level role. Leaders must continue to challenge the status quo, take more risks, and champion DEI without ostracizing their existing teams.

TAKEAWAY: *C-level leaders need to check their biases and eliminate nice-to-haves from the hiring process to remove the barrier for women and underrepresented people who have not historically sat in the C-suite. Leaders must continue to challenge the status quo, take more risks, and champion DEI without ostracizing their existing teams.*

Measuring results

Metrics will help you objectively gauge your progress on DEI efforts over time. Even if your DEI objective is as straightforward as "hire more diverse talent and increase our results from last year," you must understand how to gauge the success of your efforts.

KPI examples

Here are some examples of common metrics that businesses can use to learn what they're doing right (so they can do more of that) and what can be improved.

Recruiting

To evaluate diversity in the hiring practices, there are two areas to note in your DEI data:

- A trained, diverse hiring panel
- Diversity of the candidate pool

Both elements are crucial to make sure you draw in a vast pool of individuals with a range of histories, racial backgrounds, gender identities, sexual orientations, and more. The employment process is fairer and freer of unconscious bias when the hiring committee and human resources department are diverse.

Representation

While it's essential to draw in a wide pool of individuals with a range of histories, racial backgrounds, gender, etc., it's also important to have a diverse staff overall, including senior management.

If this isn't the case in your organization, take the time to evaluate the current situation, identify your shortcomings, and develop a strategic plan to make improvements to increase the representation of historically underrepresented groups.

Note that if you are bringing in slates of diverse candidates in your talent pool, but the diversity of your hiring and workforce is not increasing, there may be bias in the hiring processes or potential issues with retention. In some cases, you may successfully hire diverse talent at the lower levels of the organization, but your senior management is not diverse and mostly homogeneous, cisgender majority males.

Collecting demographic information on your workforce gives you a better chance of identifying issues. Is the problem with the talent pipeline, interviewing, or something else?

Is there a problem with your leadership team, onboarding, or potential system bias that needs to be addressed? Having the data will enable you to make necessary adjustments to make progress on your DEI goals.

Retention

You shouldn't just randomly hire members of underrepresented groups without a plan for how to onboard, grow, and retain them. Businesses that genuinely value DEI are intentional about creating an environment for people to be their best selves and do their best work which ultimately increases employee retention and reduces attrition.

It is imperative to measure employee turnover and attrition to determine whether your company fosters a sense of inclusivity and belonging among employees from different backgrounds.

It's a fact that employees who don't feel at home in a company will leave at a higher rate than employees who feel they belong. Allow the data to tell the story, and work with your workforce to tell the rest of the story and create an action plan for future success.

Career growth

Your diversity efforts are ineffective if there aren't enough members of underrepresented groups in your leadership. Minority groups within the firm should be clearly represented in management, including outside the C-suite.

If only members of one group receive promotions, there may be a problem with the corporate culture that must be resolved. Similarly to this, if employees from all categories aren't taking advantage of opportunities for learning and growth, it's time to address the causes.

Your work as a company committed to DEI doesn't cease after you have a diverse workforce. Their success and eventual ascent up the corporate ladder is the goal.

Employee satisfaction

Keep an eye out for which employees exhibit a higher level of job satisfaction and which ones don't. Examine the diversity statistics to determine if the dissatisfied workers are a part of any particular group.

It's time to take a step back and reevaluate your organization's culture if employee satisfaction scores are low for diverse staff. Check to see if any particular cultural concerns, such as microaggressions, are the cause of these employees feeling excluded.

Accessibility

Your DEI efforts need to focus on accessibility. Check to see if your workplace is accessible to everyone so that every employee feels included.

You can check accessibility by asking the following questions:

- Are all areas of the office physically accessible to all employees?
- Do all employees have access to a relaxing restroom?
- Do you provide enough paternity leave in addition to maternity leave?
- Do you have screen readers and other necessary equipment for employees with disabilities?
- Do you recognize and allow employees to celebrate all religious and cultural holidays?

Equity of pay

Equal pay for equal work is one of the most important topics in DEI.

Analyze your company's compensation practices, looking for any potential gaps. Then, develop ways to close the gap.

These are just some of the KPIs that your organization can use that will deliver insight into the progress you're making on your DEI journey.

Transparency

Companies need to be transparent. The goal as a company should be to get to the place where you hear people say, all the time, that they love working for this company because they're one of the best places to work.

If you want to be an authentic company that people love working for it's important to be transparent, and to be real. You've got to start at a baseline. You've got to create your brand and who you want to be. It would be best if you determined what values you want to communicate to the community you serve.

You need to identify and address you're community. If, for example, you're a local-based company that serves your local community, identify the community that you're talking to and attracting because even in your employment brand you want to attract applicants and candidates.

These people will be representatives of the community you're serving. Now if you're regionalized you might have a couple of different messages that you're going to share on a regional level versus a national level... ultimately the audience is bigger.

Your overall national employment brand message is going to lead the way for your regionalized branding. Your localized employment brand will then help candidates to identify, "Wow, that's a company that addresses some of the values and concerns that I have and I'm going to research them more and see if that's a place that's a fit for me."

When I look at this from a candidate perspective, a lot of candidates are stating, "You know, I have people from that company reach out to me all the time, but one of the things that I ask myself is, 'Hey, who do they hire at this company? I haven't really seen evidence that they're reaching out and trying to get with other people who look like me.'"

Everybody involved in employment branding should be thinking, "why should a candidate work for our company?" How do you answer that question? Is there a match between the values of the company and the candidate? Candidates are being much more selective about the companies they've worked for, even in times when there are lots of jobs out there, or maybe they're not that many jobs, but candidates are still thoughtful.

It's not enough anymore to just have a job. Candidates want to know if they're going to a place that values them and that they're going to a place where they can start, grow, and progress in their careers.

Sometimes candidates are just starting their careers. Therefore, they tend to focus on how deeply they connect with a particular company.

Authentic Messaging

If a company is trying to engage emotionally with consumers or potential candidates and staff they need to be authentic, and their brand needs to be consistent.

You don't want an individual to read one thing from you only to question themselves, "Hey, wait a minute, I thought you stood for this, but you're coming across totally different."

This can be considered a gaslighting marketing moment. You want to be authentic with how you communicate, whether visually or through recorded or video messages, and present yourself in a way that attracts that diverse group to you.

Candidates are seeking more and more genuine messaging from employers.

Leadership Messages

One of the things I often say is that diversity and inclusion is a "feeling, thinking, and caring mindset." So, when you're in diversity recruiting, use your head and open your heart to be successful.

Key message: inclusion is about all of us.

The key to success in building an inclusive and diverse workplace is to be intentional and work together as a team.

<u>**Valuable Points to Remember as a Leader**</u>

- ✓ You must start with the end in mind.
- ✓ Retention starts with recruiting.
- ✓ Each function is uniquely prepared to impact diversity, equity, inclusion, and belonging.
- ✓ Orientation is one day, and onboarding is ongoing.
- ✓ The end result does not happen overnight and will create some chaos as you determine your lane.
- ✓ Use insight from hiring to build the thirty-, sixty-, and ninety-day plan.
- ✓ The proper transitioning from recruiting to onboarding is key.
- ✓ Great onboarding is a team effort.

> **TIP:** *A great example of teamwork is the production of a Broadway play or motion picture.*

Everyone knows what the goal is, and they understand how their role contributes to the production. Creating an inclusive and diverse workplace is no different. Every person has a role to play, and, in the end, success comes when the team works together to achieve the goal.

Onboarding

One of the first things I tell anyone when I'm doing training with them about retention is, to get their onboarding right.

Here's why:

For example, let's say I've been hired at XYZ Company. The expectation is that I have an offer letter that genuinely represents the company.

In a significant way, I have had clear and professional communication from either my hiring manager or the recruiter. When I showed up on my first day, the orientation was amazing and represented the company well.

However, many times when you see turnover in your first sixty days, it is truly because the onboarding process was poor, and that's because:

- you did not train them well
- they did not have a mentor when they got there
- they didn't know the questions to ask; there was no training plan

All these things make a candidate feel like they've made the wrong choice, and there's no reason why a candidate would stick around anywhere past two months if the first two months have been horrible for them, right?

People want to feel like they've made a really good decision about their employment, especially in these turbulent times, and organizations need to recognize that their training and onboarding methods matter.

The First Ninety-Days

This is a crucial time in an employee's journey with your company. If you do it well, you will set them up for success.

✓ *Preboard new hires*

This is the process of keeping them engaged and helping them prepare for their first day. Some things you can do include providing them with any employee documentation you have, providing them with company swag such as a water bottle, notepad with your company logo, etc.

✓ *Complete paperwork quickly*

Give your new hires everything they need to make their first day productive, such as giving them HR paperwork ahead of time.

✓ *Get your employees involved*

Let everyone know about the new hire and encourage them to reach out and warmly welcome them.

✓ *Identify Gaps*

Speak with them and ask them where they want to be in the next twelve months, three years, and five years. Help them identify areas of knowledge that they want to improve and give them the resources they need to fill gaps in their knowledge experience.

✓ *Create Individual Development Plans*

Meet with each member of your team individually and work with them to create a personalized development plan. These plans should outline skills of the building support you're providing, such as paid training opportunities.

✓ *Create a One-on-One with the Manager and New Hire*

Meetings between a new hire and their manager or supervisor open the opportunity to build rapport. Additionally, it makes workers feel supported personally and professionally when their manager takes an interest in their success.

✓ *Sharing The Company Vision*

People love to feel as if they belong. One of the easiest ways to help your new hire feel like they are wanted in your organization is by inviting them to share in the company's vision. Link their work to the overall company mission.

Begin by differentiating your company's mission from your vision. Although your company's vision and goal are linked, they are different. They are traveling in the same direction and running parallel to one another; however, they are very different.

Think of it like this; your mission is the "how," while your vision is the "what."

✓ *Communicate your mission and core values with them.*

Although your company's vision and mission are connected, repetition is crucial to help people remember it. Eventually, it becomes engrained in their everyday routines and thought processes.

At the same time, encourage manager feedback. This can help you spot any discrepancies between what you intend to convey and what the employee actually hears.

> **NOTE:** *When recruiting, your focus should have been on matching candidates' values with those of your organization rather than company culture.*
>
> *If you were focused on values rather than "culture fit," you'll find it much easier to ensure that your new hire will clearly understand the part they play in the company's mission because they share the same vision.*

Aligning Company Needs with New Hire Needs

Expectations are a normal component of human nature when entering any environment, and the job is no exception. Naturally, you and your employees have expectations about what you want from them and what you will provide for them. It's important to strike the correct balance between the two sets of expectations because relationships are a two-way street.

If you don't think about and consider the expectations of everyone involved your business may face difficulties. The bottom line, addressing any unrealistic or erroneous expectations up front is critical before they become an issue.

Development Plan

During the debrief, recruiters and hiring managers know what candidates will do well. There are also instances where you're bringing a candidate on, and you're like, "Hey, we don't think they have 'X' fully, but this is a skill that they can develop, or this is a competency that we need to develop and pay attention to."

In that situation, you can add that to their development plan.

Unfortunately, a lot of organizations aren't doing this, so they're letting skilled talent slip through their fingers by not doing a good job onboarding them.

Training And Development

Does your company allow for any professional development? Is there a tuition reimbursement program? Are your employees allowed to take any type of soft skills training or virtual webinars? Are you allowing them to have LinkedIn Learning Accounts that you pay for?

If you're not doing any of these things you cannot expect your employees to get better if they are always trying to tackle the fires in front of them, and then trying to figure out "how do I close the gap on things that I can't do?"

This is why it's important if you come across someone who is just short of having the skills you need, but is still a great choice, you pass along this information to the hiring manager, who needs to add this to the person's onboarding plan.

This one thing could make a huge difference in retention. Keeping the practices in this section top of mind will help you leverage some of the best practices and approaches to building an impactful DEI strategy, no matter how large or small your organization may be.

Inclusion Statement

Developing an inclusion statement for a company focused on creating a diverse and inclusive workplace involves several key steps. Here's a suggested process to follow:

- Assemble a diverse team: Form a team with a mix of backgrounds, experiences, and perspectives to ensure a comprehensive understanding of the company's values and goals regarding diversity and inclusion.
- Conduct research: Gather information on best practices, industry standards, and legal requirements for diversity and inclusion. Research other organizations' inclusion statements for inspiration and learn from their successes and challenges.
- Assess current status: Conduct an internal assessment to understand the current state of diversity and inclusion within the company. This may include employee surveys, focus groups, or interviews to gather insights on employee experiences and perspectives.
- Define key principles: Collaborate with your team to identify the core principles that will guide your inclusion statement. These principles should be rooted in the company's values and should reflect its commitment to fostering a diverse and inclusive environment.
- Draft the statement: Begin writing the inclusion statement, incorporating your key principles, research findings, and employee input. Ensure the language is clear, concise, and inclusive, avoiding jargon and buzzwords.
- Solicit feedback: Share the draft with stakeholders, including employees, leadership, and external partners, to gather their input and suggestions. This feedback will help ensure the statement resonates with all members of the company community and aligns with the organization's goals.
- Revise and refine: Incorporate the feedback you receive to revise and refine the statement. This process may require multiple iterations to ensure the statement accurately represents the company's commitment to diversity and inclusion.

- Obtain leadership approval: Present the final draft of the inclusion statement to the company's leadership team for review and approval. Their support and endorsement will be critical to the success of your diversity and inclusion initiatives.
- Communicate and implement: Share the approved inclusion statement with all employees, emphasizing its importance and relevance to the company's mission and values. Use various communication channels, such as internal newsletters, team meetings, and the company website, to ensure widespread dissemination.
- Monitor and update: Periodically evaluate the effectiveness of the inclusion statement and its impact on the company culture. Make adjustments and updates as needed to ensure it remains relevant and aligned with the organization's evolving goals and priorities.

CHAPTER FOUR

CULTURE FIT VS. VALUES

In this chapter, we will go into detail on why it's important not to hire for culture fit. Instead, hire for culture adds. Hiring for culture fit will impede your DEI efforts as it's subjective and means something different to everyone.

Instead, hire for values, competencies, skills, and behaviors. When hiring for core values, it is important to ensure that everyone on the interview team understands the intended meaning of each core value and the behaviors associated with each core value. It also helps to ensure that people understand the implications and outcomes when the core value is not lived up to and how that impacts the company and the organization. Asking behavioral questions that address each core value and listen to how the candidate has demonstrated the core value in their past experiences.

Much of your ability to influence is going to come as the result of your ability to get your hiring teams to hire for values, skills, and competencies versus culture fit. Also, consider what your must-haves are versus your nice-to-haves when it comes to filling open roles.

The recruiting industry, like most industries, uses a lot of buzzwords. And I'll wager that one of the expressions you've heard around the topic of diversity recruiting is culture fit. While culture fit may appear to be a reliable indicator for hiring individuals with diverse backgrounds, it isn't.

If you want your diversity efforts to be effective, I recommend you remove culture fit from your hiring process. Using culture fit as a recruiting factor can result in a great candidate being passed over solely because decision-makers felt the candidate "wasn't a culture match."

Now, I'm not saying eliminate your company's culture. Not at all. Instead, I prefer to look at the concept through a different lens. Drop that phrase from your lexicon if you want to enhance your capacity to identify outstanding individuals. Instead, assess candidates on the principles and qualities of your business values.

Culture Add VS Culture Fit

Hiring for "culture add" will increase the capability of an organization or a team and push it to not become stagnant by only hiring for a culture-fit blueprint.

Think about it. Your company's culture probably developed through time and is made up of people who are extremely similar to one another. Therefore, attempting to preserve that culture will undermine your efforts to promote diversity, equity, inclusion, and belonging.

For instance, let's say that you consistently hired the football team captain from a top-ten university for a particular position. Then, every time you interview a candidate who doesn't have that specific history, you run the risk of bias.

Why? Because it can inspire somebody to think, "Hey, this person is different. They don't match the culture." So don't believe it couldn't happen—it frequently does—often in subtle ways.

As the recruiting manager, you are in a good position to recognize unconscious bias and set an example of behavior that will transform the way you hire. Hire for the qualities and values you want to see in your firm rather than for culture fit.

Diversity Is Not Homogenous

The concept of diversity means different. So, when you employ diverse talent, it brings individuals to the table who are unique and who contribute to your existing culture.

Although it can be challenging for recruiting managers to accept change, doing so will change your organization's culture and enable you to be more inclusive. People that feel like they belong in your business can be found by fostering a culture like this. Additionally, it allows you the chance to guarantee fairness and a level playing field for all parties.

Change is necessary. It entails risk. And building a diverse workforce where everyone can feel appreciated with a sense of belonging to the organization requires persistence and enthusiasm.

Bias Awareness

I mentioned bias earlier. There are some things the hiring manager may do to lessen bias in the hiring process.

First, be aware that bias exists in all situations. One thing you may do as a recruiting manager is to look for expert assistance. There is nothing wrong with asking for assistance in identifying and evaluating your biases.

Then, coach your teams on how to counteract that bias. First, they must be made aware of it to overcome it while evaluating talent throughout the interview process.

Hiring for values rather than culture fit is an effective strategy to overcome any biases. By doing this, you can be sure that you're treating everyone fairly and leveling the playing field.

Evaluate The Landscape

Hiring managers are uniquely positioned to influence diversity, equity, inclusion, and belonging inside their organizations. As a leader in your organization, you must seek clarification to evaluate the landscape.

What are your current diversity and inclusion efforts? Why is diversity a major focal point?

Follow up with more questions:

- What's working?
- What challenges are we having?

- Do we have leadership buy-in? If so, how? What are they doing, specifically, to help? (e.g., providing resources for your DEI efforts, etc.)

The Role of Inclusion

When talking about improving diversity efforts, the word "inclusion" is frequently used, but what is it, and why is it so crucial?

When diverse employees feel they can:

- Use their voice.
- Participate in decision-making within a group.
- Boost their standing or authority within a group.
- Feel like they truly belong and that their contribution is recognized, a workplace is considered to be inclusive.

According to Deloitte, "A growing body of research indicates that diverse and inclusive teams outperform their peers."

Businesses with inclusive talent practices in hiring, promoting, developing, leading, and team management outperform their competitors in terms of revenue per employee and profitability by up to 30 percent. The team-centric approach, which consists of diverse people, may not function well without a strong culture of inclusiveness and adaptability. Businesses must foster an inclusive environment if they wish to increase their diversity hiring efforts.

This can be accomplished by:

- Educating their leadership and staff
- Working diligently to improve communication
- Encouraging workers to be their true, authentic selves

Try Different Things

As a hiring manager, you have the ability to take some chances. Talk with your recruiter about it or bring ideas to the table, and take a chance if you're working together on initiatives that could improve your diversity and inclusion recruiting efforts.

It would be best if you took the lead. However, hiring managers occasionally lack sufficient knowledge of diversity, equity, or inclusion; if this applies to you, my best advice would be to understand the language.

Although new terms are always emerging, once you are familiar with them, step out to support your company's diversity and inclusion efforts and encourage participation across the organization.

Develop Leaders

To develop leaders who can foster a diverse and inclusive work environment, it's important to recognize the significant impact that diversity has on a company's financial success. Creating a diverse, inclusive and equitable organization takes time and resourcing but is worth the investment. Diversity has been shown to improve financial results. Businesses in the S&P 500 increased by 19.45 percent at year's end in 2017. There were no women in the C-suite or on the boards of sixteen companies at the time. Every company had at least one woman on their board by the end of 2019, which was roughly a 30 percent increase from the previous year. Simply put, having a diverse leadership team is excellent for business.

Why, then, are women and people of color still so underrepresented in senior leadership if the data is so conclusive?

The diversity recruitment firm Mogul, hosted a webinar on the subject titled "Diversity in Executive Search." Members of Mogul gained knowledge from Cathrin Stickney, the founder and CEO of Parity.org, a non-profit organization that promotes the representation of women and people of color at the highest levels of business.

She described how establishing organizational leadership parity is a multifaceted process and emphasized the significance of progressing across representation. A crucial first step in boosting representation is recruitment. There are five easily implementable executive recruitment methods that you can use to increase your chances of hiring the greatest people if you're in leadership and hoping to diversify your staff, which you should be.

1. Eliminate unconscious bias at every opportunity.
2. Be deliberate in your recruiting process.
3. Put together a diverse interview panel.
4. Hold your search firm or recruiter accountable.
5. Be aware of common myths and see through them.

Creating leaders is another method recruiting managers may use to promote their talent goals. This implies that you might occasionally be placing someone in a situation for which they may not be adequately qualified.

I don't necessarily mean a job position; rather, I'm referring to a project or a task, particularly for those individuals who demonstrate a desire and motivation to accept such a big challenge.

Interviewer Capability

As a recruiting manager and company leader, make sure the right people are participating in your interviews, and are adequately prepared.

Bring experienced interviewers to the table. This can occasionally present issues because an experienced interviewer might not be an inclusive and skilled interviewer.

Therefore, if you want to be sure that your interview team is capable of evaluating diverse talent, make sure that:

- The interviewers have received inclusive interviewer training.
- You are aware of the questions that interviewers are asking, and no one is asking the unfair questions that they've been asking for the

last five, six, seven, or even twenty years that might not be relevant to the job or to candidates in the current job market.

Interview Tips

You might want to reconsider your interview strategy if you're still interviewing candidates the same way you did fifteen or twenty years ago where the focus was on hiring for culture fit.

Make sure you have a model in place that allows you to evaluate the applicant's values, skills, and competencies. For instance, if your interview team is homogeneous and everyone comes from similar backgrounds , and you interview a candidate with a different and nontraditional background, you might not get the response you're expecting in terms of cadence, language, or tone. With such an unexpected response you'll "no-hire" the candidate.

I've observed this happening in numerous organizations over a number of the years, and it wasn't always because the interviewer didn't want to employ the candidate; rather, it was because they lacked a method of evaluating the candidate, and used their gut feeling to assess the candidate instead of having a structured way to evaluate the candidate.

Interviewer Tools

I recommend using structured interviews to give companies the tools and plans to guide the interview process. I also recommend preparing interviewers to use a framework for asking questions.

The framework that I use most commonly is on the next page. It's called "SPARKLE."

Story
Problem
Action
Results
Know
Lessons
Evidence

The "S" in SPARKLE stands for what's the story.

This acronym was created for a behavioral interviewer. For example, "Tell me about a moment when you had to resolve a challenging client issue."

When utilizing SPARKLE, you keep an ear out for possible candidates to share their experiences.

The "P" is for the problem.

What problem were they trying to solve?

The "A" is for action.

What action did the candidate take to solve the problem?

The "R" stands for results.

What are the results that they achieved from those actions?

The "K" is for knowledge.

What does the candidate know now that they didn't know then, and how would they make adjustments to their efforts?

The "L" stands for lessons.

What are the lessons learned, and how would they apply those lessons in a future effort or a future problem?

And the "E" is for evidence.

What evidence do they have today that says, their actions were successful and had the impact they wanted?

Even though *SPARKLE* is a bit lengthy and/or complex, it allows you to dig deeper.

How To Use SPARKLE With an Applicant

The tendency of an interviewer is to dismiss a candidate who partially answers a question and move on to the next one if they do so. I encourage you to question the candidate if they didn't provide you with enough information about their actions.

Ask them something along the lines of, "Hey, tell me more about that. Help me understand more of what you're sharing. What did this experience teach you? What do you know today that you wish you had known when you first started out? What proof do you have that what you just said is factual or actually works?"

This is one way to keep digging into the candidate's answers. The other thing you can do as a manager is to ensure that your interviewees are varied and that you are highlighting.

And when discussing diversity, I don't just mean gender, race, or ethnicity. If your business lacks diversity in terms of race, gender, disability, neurodiversity, sexual orientation, or any visible or non-visible aspect of diversity, look for individuals with unconventional viewpoints and include them in the interview process.

Having diversity of viewpoints in your interview will be helpful with your inclusive approach. It will put you in a better position to assess a candidate and determine whether you want to bring them to the table because they share your values, rather than determining whether they will or won't fit into your company's culture.

Role Requirements

You should also have a look at the qualifications for the role. You want to employ the best candidate with the right set of talents for the position. Additionally, we overload job descriptions with too many qualifications that aren't truly requirements to do the job and are often unnecessary for the role.

Decide what the minimum requirements are for the position and prioritize the must-haves for the role. Given the pressure to hire unicorns and superstars, we often add every nice-to-have skill and competency that we can think of to recruit that "Rockstar" person. We want to maximize every hiring opportunity and find the greatest candidate we can find, but some of the abilities we're searching for might not be necessary for that particular role, so prioritize the role requirements and focus on the must-haves for the job.

Unconscious Bias

Companies frequently exclude candidates who would support their efforts to hire more diversely. Businesses frequently don't realize what hinders them from boosting their diversity hiring efforts because they are so focused on finding someone to fill a position.

For instance, the business I work with has been operational for more than forty years. They are attempting to diversify the executive leadership position. But they weren't aware that they were eliminating candidates if they lacked certain characteristics because all of the present executives attended a particular institution, had a certain GPA, and engaged in certain activities whether it was five or fifteen years ago.

Simply because they weren't from the same school, had different experiences, etc., they weren't even giving these varied individuals an opportunity to interview or to exhibit the success that they've had.

Screening "in" Not Screening "out"

Finally, change the way you consider candidates for employment. Start "screening in" prospects rather than "screening out." It's a small distinction, but screening out a candidate implies that you're looking for a justification to say no and that the applicant must convince the employer to say yes.

Therefore, having this perspective greatly affects your capacity to recruit talent that is diverse from the talent you already have. The culture fit question is strongly related to the entire screening out idea. Therefore, companies should be more open-minded and look for ways to identify the positive aspects that a person brings to the table rather than screening out people. As a result, businesses will be better able to increase their diversity hiring.

Competitive Advantage of An Inclusive Culture of Recruiting

Here are some ways that inclusive workplaces give businesses a competitive advantage.

It reduces employee turnover

Businesses are successful in keeping the talent that they worked so hard to get in the first place. People are more likely to stick with an organization if they believe they may advance their careers and that their ideas are valued.

Additionally, it enables the business to explain how individuals who potentially resemble the target audience fit into their organization and how they support their overall business plan.

It increases engagement

People will be more engaged if they believe their efforts are valued and have an impact on both the company's and each employee's performance.

This is due to the fact that everyone who works there feels appreciated and contributes to the telling of the company's story.

It ensures scalability

When it comes to hiring or retention, having an inclusive recruiting culture will enable you to require each employee to contribute to the talent pool.

This is more scalable than attempting to create a large recruiting team or a team just responsible for recruiting diversity. The bottom line is affected by having this inclusive culture since your business can now focus on what it has to do for its clients and customers.

It transcends your organization

Your brand, your goods, and of course, your people all contribute to an inclusive recruiting culture that extends beyond the confines of your company.

All these factors will reveal whether or not your market solutions were created with inclusion in mind. They will demonstrate whether your market research, product development, and other processes—from the design phase to the marketing—taking into account your entire target market.

As a result, when businesses interested in partnering with your organization look at what you're doing, they will see that your words and actions are consistent; which is undoubtedly a potent factor that can encourage them to get in touch with your business.

The topics in this chapter will help you take the necessary steps to hire for desired values, skills, and behaviors in your organization and will ultimately impact the customers you serve.

Hiring based on values instead of hiring for culture fit gives you a competitive advantage and will help your organization grow the right way. This won't be easy, but in the end, you will appreciate the success that you see from removing culture fit from the interview process.

PART III
ROLES

"The question isn't who is going to let me. It's who is going to stop me."
~ Ayn Rand

CHAPTER FIVE

ROLES IN BUILDING AN INCLUSIVE RECRUITING CULTURE

To have an effective diversity recruiting strategy, it's important to define—and understand—the impact that roles have on your DEI-building efforts. It's imperative to understand the role of talent acquisition, of HR, the hiring manager, and each employee in the organization.

The function of each role needs to be uniquely prepared to impact diversity, equity, inclusion, and belonging. And be prepared to have uncomfortable conversations about implicit bias, race, and gender issues.

You want to be able to take advantage of getting your employees engaged and really having them understand their roles in the entire recruiting process. Therefore you must start internally with your team and grow that capability inside your business.

Do Your Employees Feel Connected to Your Company's Vision?

Many times, you hear people use sports analogies about teams, but one of the things that I think about is the organization you see when people are producing a movie or a play.

You have actors, the supporting cast, and everyone knows what their role is and they're all focused on getting that movie out or producing that play.

This is what happens when you get your employees involved in recruiting from a perspective where they all know what their role in the process is and what their jobs are. You have to empower them.

Having an internal focus on your commitment to diversity, inclusion, equity, and belonging, where everyone discusses the importance, will actually help people become more focused and it will lead to everyone having an emotional connection to your vision and mission.

Talent Acquisition's Role

Commit to DIEB (Diversity, Inclusion, Equity and, Belonging)

Building an inclusive recruiting environment and recruiting internally first are two ways recruiters may ensure that employment openings are promoted and discussed within. Creating a culture of inclusive hiring includes motivating employees, and there is nothing more motivating than seeing their career progress.

Expand our thinking

Additionally, as recruiters, we regularly go out and meet new people to develop relationships. We can use this practice to help us encourage other people to do the same thing.

Consider the case where you have a group of engineers. They aren't recruiters, but you can teach them skills that will make it easier for them to interact with people and build some of the connections you need. Just share the basics, they don't have to become as outgoing as many recruiters are, but they can make connections with their peers and others who share common backgrounds and experiences to start the relationships which may lead to finding your next great hire.

After all, as a talent acquisition leader, you should want to know the talent before you ever know about the opportunity, right?

Interviewer capability

The talent acquisition team can support interviewer competency by assisting individuals in recognizing potential bias and offering techniques (such as providing an interviewer toolkit) for minimizing its effects.

Just make sure the interviewers are aware of their roles when they become involved and that your efforts are pertinent and current to what you're attempting to achieve with an inclusive workforce.

Offer bias training

Provide implicit bias and awareness training, as well as instruction on how to interview candidates. The talent acquisition team has a variety of options at its disposal, like using a more diverse group of interviewers who may be more able to connect with some of the applicants.

Career development

Are people able to go out and tell your company's story and more importantly can they tell their story to other people to help attract people and talent to the organization?

How do you talk to candidates about the work that you do and not only that, how do we talk to other people inside of the organization who are aspiring to get to certain roles?

It always starts with their story … how they came to be with the brand and the career they've been able to develop while working with your organization. The goal is to create connection … every person needs to see themselves as a hero playing a part in the story that is your business and your vision. More importantly, they need to see examples where people have advanced to the highest levels in your organization allowing them to see that, "Hey, I can grow my career here because Jill started where I am and now she's VP of sales."

Values-focused (not culture fit)

Your company culture should evolve, not stay the same. That's why, when you hire according to values rather than some arbitrary concept of culture, you're able to match people from all backgrounds who will bring their culture with them.

This is a more inclusive, natural way to build a diverse workforce.

People-focused (not process or product focused)

Again, think of ways to screen in rather than screen out candidates. Research has shown that people develop the best and the fastest when they have a rich set of on-the-job experiences.

So what does that mean? Instead of having requirements that screen out potential hires, focus on creating requirements and processes that screen in candidates. This increases your ability to attract—and retain—diverse individuals to your organization. When reviewing best-in-class talent based on potential, you improve retention because individuals are allowed to lead in their space. This drives commitment to the shared vision of your company.

Human Resources Role

In addition to what I've already shared above, HR needs to:

- ☐ Help leaders lead
- ☐ Present demographics data
- ☐ Increase interviewer capability
- ☐ Empower business champions
- ☐ Improve bias awareness
- ☐ Communicate legal considerations
- ☐ Share good practices versus risky practices
- ☐ Measure hires, promotions, retention

Hiring Manager's Role

In addition to what I've talked about throughout this chapter, the hiring manager can help with your organization's DEI efforts when they:

- Probe candidates, stick with the candidate, and listen for transferrable skills
- Take job-related notes, and provide legally defensible feedback
- Be prepared for the interview, read the resume, and understand the job description/responsibilities if applicable
- Address inappropriate or irrelevant information volunteered by candidates by stating that "That is not information that we will need in making a hiring decision," or "feel free to follow up with the recruiter regarding that question/concern."
- Don't tell the candidate that he/she will be employed by your company

Employee Engagement (cast and crew mindset)

It stands repeating that … every person in the organization can play a part in building a diverse workforce. The key is to ensure that every person in the company knows how they contribute to the recruiting culture.

It's like the cast and support crew for a movie or play. Every person needs to understand how their role supports the performance.

What actions can your employees take to get started? Encourage them to:

- Think about how they can make a difference.
- Make sure they know about the opportunities within the organization that they might be interested in, or that someone they know might be interested in.
- Be intentional and own it.
- Provide the resources to go out there and make connections and network. For example, if there's a special networking event with an organization or an alma mater that is coming up, give them the time and resources if needed, to get out there and represent your company.
- Start with the end in mind by having them visualize the workplace that they want to see. Who did they go to school with?

- Who do they socialize with?
- Who have they met at a conference?
- Who have they worked with on a project?

Also:

- Who do you know from a distance who may not look like you?
- Ask questions.
- Research diversity and inclusion in your profession.
- Engage with organizations focused on diversity.
- Find schools, networks, and organizations by searching.

Talent Scouting

Talent scouting is a long-term, proactive approach to recruiting. It's about engaging talent proactively rather than reactively. You're proactively building relationships before you have a job opportunity.

After you've been working on building rapport and getting to know top diverse talent, when a position opens you can quickly have a slate of candidates who know your organization, who have the skills, and who are willing to talk about the opportunity.

Give People Freedom, Responsibility, And Accountability

Building a culture of recruiting means everyone knows their role, you give them the freedom they need to excel in that role, and you hold people accountable.

This is going to look different, depending on the roles each person holds; not everyone's going to be on the phone or doing the same thing that your recruiters are doing, but everyone's got a part and they need to know their part, be responsible, and accountable for it.

Leadership Involvement

A culture of recruiting also means that leadership needs to be involved. For example, if you're trying to land top talent and another major player in your industry is reaching out to the same person, your leaders can step in if needed to help nudge the person closer to the opportunity with you.

Select A Champion

Find someone who believes in diversity.

This is probably the most important step in the process of boosting your diversity recruiting efforts. The key is to find someone who actually believes in diversity beyond the business case for diversity.

You are going to hear many conversations and if you read anything on the internet or anything on social media, there is a wealth of information about the business case for diversity.

You'll read how diverse teams are more effective than nondiverse teams and you're also going to hear a lot about equity, inclusion, and belonging and making sure that your workplace is a place where everyone can be themselves.

If you've done any diversity recruiting before, you know it's a challenge, and especially in this market, there are many challenges, and there's lots of competition for diverse talent.

Candidates are being inundated by recruiters reaching out and talking to them and my guess is that you're probably going to be looking for the same candidates that many other small and large companies are looking for.

So, selecting a champion (who doesn't actually have to be an executive) is key.

Characteristics of a diversity champion

Here are some characteristics of what you want to look for when you're selecting that diversity champion.:

- Look at somebody who might have benefited from diversity recruiting efforts.
- Seek someone who has a diverse set of friends or interacts with many different people.
- If you find someone who is passionate about diversity, they may not have that diverse set of friends, but they may still be a great ally for your efforts. You will want to ensure that they are ready to face the resistance that comes along with championing your DEI efforts. No matter who is selected as a champion, you need to let them know that the work is part of a journey, not a destination. Giving the champion a realistic picture of the road ahead may cause them to decide that they might not have what it takes to be the champion. When it gets tough you need someone who really believes in what you're trying to accomplish with your DEI recruiting efforts.
- Search for someone who's going to be a relationship builder and listener who understands that there will be more questions than answers, but they are okay with the ambiguity and they're willing to work through it with others.
- You need a DEI champion who has a level of authenticity and gravitas to help them grasp and work through the serious challenges of leading your DEI efforts.

One of the keys to getting talent to engage is relationships, so you want someone who can go out, establish relationships, and spend time with the people you're trying to recruit.

The champion should be engaging, resourceful, driven, and focused, ideally, someone who can handle problems by soliciting for ideas and solutions from diverse groups of people inside and outside of your organization. All these attributes are going to help your efforts take off much quicker than they would if you were just working from a cookie-cutter playbook.

Diversity Recruiting

Diversity has many dimensions, but there are two major areas of focus in diversity recruiting.

Organizational Culture

There's the cultural work that happens internally at a company where you're trying to establish an inclusive environment so people can be who they say they want to be and feel like they belong in the organization. The organizational culture work is critical to the overall company's success. It shapes the way employees behave and interact with each other, and it can have a significant impact on the company's performance. Inclusive and consistent organizational culture work will greatly improve your diversity recruiting success, and will create a positive culture for the benefit of everyone.

Talent Acquisition

The other part of diversity recruiting is talent acquisition. I tend to focus more on this subject. How do you identify the talent? How do you find the talent, and how do you get them engaged?

It's valuable to know how to recruit, so you need someone who understands the recruiting world and:

- The difficulty of finding and assessing talent.
- The complexity of competing with other companies who are looking for the same rare talent.
- The experience working with cross-functional internal stakeholders and external organizations.

They may be a senior person, or they may be more junior, but you're looking for the characteristics pertaining to the ability to drive and lead many efforts. Ultimately you want someone with a wide range of experiences

An enormous part of working in this space and trying to recruit talent would be overcoming some of the challenges and having insight and visibility into matters other than just recruiting for the roles that you're presently recruiting on.

So, if you can find someone who has those attributes or experiences, it will boost your diversity recruiting efforts. It's also going to give you the passionate person behind working on your diversity efforts because as anyone who's done diversity recruiting knows, this is a challenging space to be in.

It's much easier just to put a person in a seat than it is to make sure that you're providing that diverse slate of talent. You need a champion with the tenacity and commitment to stand up to resistance and setbacks along your diversity recruiting journey. Your DEI champion will play a major role in building an inclusive culture of recruiting. Selecting the right person is critical to the overall success of your DEI journey.

PART IV

STEERING AND FRAMEWORK

*"Sometimes we are blessed with being able to choose
the time, and the arena, and the manner of our revolution,
but more usually
we must do battle where we are standing."*
~ Audre Lorde

CHAPTER SIX

ENTERPRISE RELATIONSHIP FRAMEWORK

An enterprise relationship framework will position your company for greater success by recruiting and hiring a diverse workforce. This chapter will provide the key elements, criteria, and approach to creating and operationalizing a framework for your diversity recruiting strategy.

Start With the End in Mind

The first thing you want to do with your diversity recruiting efforts is really to start with the end in mind. Create your vision and ask yourself, what does success look like and what do you need to be successful?

Next, Put Milestones in Your Plan

People talk about having S.M.A.R.T. goals and metrics, but first, you need to be able to define what success looks like and develop your own measurements of what success looks like for your organization and you personally. You can't always use every metric that you use in the recruiting industry or borrow metrics from other companies, so you will need to give this some thought.

Your metrics should be tailored to your organization, so invest the time to visualize what success is going to look like for your organization from a diversity perspective.

Building A Framework

The reason behind building a framework for your diversity recruiting efforts is to help you support and prioritize your selection and decision-making along the way. As soon as you say, "Hey, we've got an initiative, or we've got an effort to increase diversity," Ideas will not trickle in but flood the gates.

People will produce many ideas on what you should do when creating a strategy. They're going to come up with many places to visit, including schools and organizations that you can participate in, and relationships that you should be building.

You will also receive ideas from your workforce and leaders, but you need to have the ability to decide which organizations you're going to work with because to be successful, you've got to take this as a step-by-step approach.

Anyone can brainstorm ideas for a strategy, but few people will know how to operationalize the strategy to achieve your desired results. You must slow down to speed up. Small wins over a longer period will help you achieve success because there's a lot of learning that's going to take place.

You don't want to stymie someone's enthusiasm, so you need a way of prioritizing and letting people know what you look for when you're looking for an organization, or a school to participate in.

*Here is a general outline for your framework.
I will discuss each element of the framework
throughout this chapter.*

Establish Your Criteria for Why You Would Engage An Organization.

You will need to select the criteria that work for your organization to decide why you would partner with each organization. For example, below are some common criteria that companies may use:

Branding and credibility

A lot of organizations will use branding and credibility as criteria.

So, if you say hey, we're going to interact with this organization and if we interact with them, we have to have the opportunity to show our brand and to showcase our credibility as a great employer.

Hiring and recruiting

Maybe hiring and recruiting are other criteria that you plan on using. Take the time to determine whether you're going to participate in that organization. If the organization doesn't have a component that allows you to hire or recruit talent, it might not be the right organization to work for at that time.

Professional development may be another thing that you're looking at

You want your workforce to have the opportunity to get professional development while they are participating with this organization.

Showcase your social responsibility

Then, you may want to showcase your social responsibility or your corporate responsibility so that the candidates understand more about your organization. When you're trying to decide which way to go, I wouldn't make a huge list to work with. Instead create a list of three to five criteria items to utilize when deciding whether or not to engage an organization. This will be an excellent place for you to begin.

When you receive the list of a hundred different places that you should go, you will have a way to decide what makes sense: they meet three or five of our criteria or they meet all five or they meet two. You'll have to decide on the guidelines with your organization.

The example criteria described above are just samples of what you might use for your criteria.

Select the criteria that makes sense in your organization.

> **TIP:** Ask the following questions to test whether the criteria works for your company:

"Does this allow us to build our employment branding credibility?"

Many organizations will use this as criteria so if you say, "We're going to interact with this organization and if we interact with them, we have to have the opportunity to show our brand and to show our credibility as an employer."

"Does this allow us to hire and recruit?"

Maybe hiring and recruiting is another criterion that you're going to use to decide whether you're going to participate with that organization. So, if the organization doesn't have a component that allows you to hire or recruit talent it might not be the organization to engage with.

"Does this allow us to provide professional development for our employees?"

Maybe another factor that you're reviewing is the need for your workforce to have the opportunity to get professional development while participating with this organization.

"Does this allow us to show our social or corporate responsibility?"

You may want to highlight your social responsibility or your corporate responsibility so that the candidates understand more about your organization.

You may decide to use these or other criteria when you're deciding on the organizations you want to engage with. I wouldn't make a huge list but having three to five criteria items that you use to decide "why would we engage this organization" can help when you're hit with a list of a hundred different places you should go.

Create Your Approach

It's important that you create the approach that you're going to take. That said, I recommend that you take a multi-touch approach. Engage the diversity organization locally, regionally, and nationally and build relationships. In some cases, you may engage internationally.

Many times, companies will have a list of diversity organizations that they want to partner with and they decide to attend the national conference without planning ahead or preparing. The usual result is disappointment and a lower-than-expected return on investment (ROI).

For example, let's take a well-known organization, the Black MBA Association. Many brands will say, "Hey, we're going to the national conference for the National Black MBA Association." But when they get there, they realize that the candidates aren't interacting with them because the candidates don't know your brand and they're not engaged in a way that you might have hoped.

It's because you jumped a couple of steps, went straight to the national event, then walked away, thinking, "Hey, we didn't get what we were looking for out of that organization."

To be more effective and to have more impact, you need to take a multi-touch approach, so the candidates know you when you get to the national event.

There are local chapters for the National Black MBA, so get some people from your organization to engage with that organization locally. Learn a little bit about the organization and share more about your organization. By the time you get to the next step—the regional organization—they know a little bit more about you.

You will learn more at the regional organization and when you get to the national conference or the national event, they will know more about you and you will know more about them.

So, help the organizations get to know your company, your employees and your genuine focus on working with them. Touch the organizations at every opportunity. This starts with having a genuine interest in their members and their organization's mission and purpose. Make sure that they see you as a true partner, not just an employer.

Don't start by just attending the national conference. Take advantage of local, regional, and then national events. Be intentional about building relationships with the organizations, schools, alumni, and members of the community.

It's all about establishing relationships because they matter. Relationship building is not a one-time event; it is a long-term commitment to working and growing with the organization.

Here are some tips to help you work better with diversity organizations at local, regional, and national opportunities:

- Provide information about your company in advance
- Meet them where they are and provide useful professional information
- Host open houses and onsite visits
- Attend Webinars and virtual chats
- Provide scholarships, jobs, and career talks
- Introduce your employees and professionals who can talk about your company and roles
- Introduce hiring managers
- Share insight about your hiring process and company
- Host mock interview and resume review sessions

These are just a few tips to help you build trust and grow the partnerships and relationships on the journey to becoming a trusted partner.

Establish Tier Priorities

There are several methods you can use to organize your priorities list into tiers.

You may choose to call these tiers blue, gold, red, or silver. You can call it whatever you want to call it, whatever works in your culture, but the concept is that you want the ability to establish tiers to help you decide where to focus your efforts.

I will dive into more detail on establishing tiers below. For now, let's say that you have received a long list of organizations, schools, and events that your employees and leaders have recommended. What do you do?

For example, you could say, "Hey, this is a tier one organization that we've decided to participate with and the reason it's a tier one is... " Now you need an answer that makes sense, and your stakeholders aren't going to take 'just because' as an acceptable answer.

Let's say you're in product development and you pick an organization that has all the talent that could fill any of our technical roles, so you decide it's a tier-one organization, but the executive leadership team doesn't agree. What do you tell them?

As part of your framework, you need to define your tiers and educate your stakeholders on the meanings and criteria for your tiers. For now, let's just name them Tier One, Tier Two, and Tier Three.

Let's say your CEO says, "Hey, this is my alma mater and I think this would be a great organization for us to recruit from." What do you do? Tiering your relationship framework allows you to say yes to more people because it provides options and criteria for how you engage and resource each potential organization. I will go into this in more detail in this chapter.

Defining Tiers

A successful framework must provide a way for you to prioritize resources and budget. Defining tiers allows you to prioritize and explain your decisions.

For example, "Hey, we have decided to participate with this organization because it meets five out of five of our criteria, and it's a Tier One since it has a company-wide strategic value and has talent available that all our divisions can hire."

Tier One – Company Wide

The people, the candidates, and the talent in this organization are people that match all, or a high percentage of, our functional areas.

For example, you may be in IT, in Marketing, in HR, or wherever, and you're going to pick an organization that has all the talent that could fill any of those roles. With this Tier One organization, you may decide that means we will provide funding, people, and corporate-wide engagement and branding ... whatever is needed for us to work with this Tier One organization.

Tier Two – Divisional

A Tier Two might be an organization that is specifically focused on one division of your organization. For example, accounting and finance.

This organization might not have the talent you're looking for company-wide, but they have the talent for the finance and accounting department.

That's why the finance and accounting departments will provide funding and other resources. This will help them move the needle with that organization and build relationships.

Tier Three – Opportunistic

And then, finally, Tier Three.

We all have Tier Three organizations in our lives. It might be an organization that you said, "Hey, this is my alma mater, or it's our CEO's alma mater. They don't have the talent that we're looking for typically, and there's no strategic reason why we should be engaged other than the fact that the CEO wants to participate and thinks it is important."

So, you want a way for the CEO to have a process for submitting people who are identified as candidates into your recruiting process while not spending lots of resources from the company to support it.

For example, it's the annual event that your CEO goes to every year at their junior college. There's nothing wrong with the junior college, but this school may not have what you're looking for in all the divisions of your company.

But you want a way to support the people who are going. Therefore, offer advice, steps, procedures, and possibly collateral that will allow them to represent your company the right way.

You wouldn't dedicate and allocate lots of company resources for this particular event. By tiering this, it allows you to say "yes" to more people because if you decided to limit the number of organizations and limit the number of schools that you're going to engage in from a Tier One perspective, you would still have a way to allow people to engage in other organizations and do it in a way that's consistent with what you're trying to do as a company.

Establish Internal Structure

The last part of this framework is structure—you need a structure to work internally and cross-functionally. There are several internal groups and stakeholders in your company who care about your DEI efforts.

In this case, I'll use an example of three different groups that you may establish for your organization:.

1. A Steering committee

A steering committee, or working group, or whatever you choose to call it within your organization will hold the responsibility of looking broadly across your company. Establish flexibility within your framework so there is an opportunity to bring in fresh ideas and do different things. You want the steering committee to be able to collect the best practices and share those across the company.

Typically, this group focuses on assessing compliance, the overall company effort, governance, budget, and shared learning across the company. Be sure to include broad representation on the steering committee and include people who are representing employee resource groups, managers, learning and development, men, women, recruiters, early-in-career professionals, and other stakeholders. This group collectively shares ideas that are going to get socialized and standardized across your company.

Note: I will detail this important part of your structure in the next chapter.

2. Functional core teams
3. Engagement teams

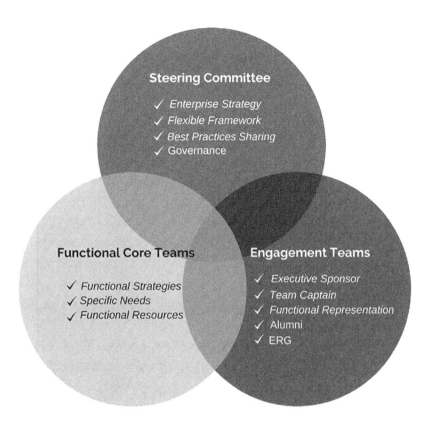

Functional Core Teams

In this yellow circle is the functional core team.

So, for example, IT may have its own group, marketing may have its own group, the finance team may have its own group, etc. But the Divisional Council sits in that division, and they're focused on making things work for that organization and that group.

The finance team may be trying to increase the representation of women, Asians, Hispanics, African-Americans, or whatever demographic they're working on. They've identified places that they're going to go; some of those places may be on your Tier One list of organizations you're going to engage in, and some may only be on Tier Two or Tier Three, but they're going to provide those functional resources, dollars, and people to support their efforts. They will communicate with the steering group and communicate anything that is working and/or challenges they're having.

Engagement Teams

The red circle represents the engagement teams. The engagement teams are the actual "boots on the ground" individuals. There may be people from the finance group, human resources, engineering, marketing, or other functional areas represented as the engagement team. This team will go to local, regional, and national events.

There's an executive sponsor who has a seat at the table with the steering committee and has a good relationship with the other functional teams. You may have a team captain if you have a variety of schools or a small number of schools or more\less organizations that will help organize and coordinate the efforts that happen on the ground.

The functional representation may be coming from all of the various business groups and lines of businesses within your organization.

You may also have alumni from:

- particular schools,
- particular organizations,
- people from your employee resource groups (ERGs).

These are the individuals who come from diverse populations within your organization and want to be an active part of these engagement teams. When you show up at the event, you will have people who look like and have similar backgrounds to the people you're trying to recruit.

This part of the framework is about enhancing your internal communication, coordination, and teamwork so everyone is on the same page, and best practices get shared across the organization. This helps the company solve challenges and share those solutions and practices across the organization.

Now that you have "boots on the ground" helping your engagement teams, go out and represent the company well.

The engagement team should be allowed to operate within a high-level framework that outlines the strategies you'll use when attempting to engage organizations to build your workforce.

Remember …

- People "buy" when they know, like, and trust you!
- Know key areas of focus and criteria, and define your purpose.
- Build brand and credibility.
- Attract and hire.
- Demonstrate corporate and social responsibility.
- Showcase your company and its people.
- People need to think about why they're doing it. What are the key focus areas that they're trying to make an impact in?
- Specifically, what's the criteria for deciding what organizations and schools to engage as a company, then what approach do you take?

ERGs in Your Recruiting Efforts

You've heard the saying, "Sitting on a gold mine." It's used to describe when someone has access to something precious but they don't know it. This is true for recruiting leaders. They often develop marketing strategies around the external, but sometimes you don't have to reach out for ideas. You can reach in.

Your team is a resource. But more specifically, when developing diversity strategies, your employee resource groups (ERGs) are the gold mines you've never considered. One of the best things you could do as the talent leader responsible for your diversity recruiting effort is to leverage your employee resource groups. When you begin to view these groups as specialized organizations within the company, you'll see their full potential. ERGs allow you to accelerate your community engagement and build relationships with other organizations to further engage with diverse communities.

Employee resource groups, also known as affinity groups, are volunteer employee-led groups centered around specific identities. These identities include black, Latinx, women, people with disabilities, neurodiversity, lgbtqia2s+, veteran, etc. There is a range of ERGs, but many companies lack thoughtfully working with their ERGs in their overall DEI recruiting efforts—to their detriment.

ERG members satisfy multiple functions, and once you realize this, you'll see the goldmine sitting right under your nose.

- They can be on-the-ground participants, attending events, being university representatives, or doing small business community outreach.
- They can also be consultants and strategists, lending their expertise and experience to marketing and branding or participating in your diversity steering or other divisional diversity committees. They are highly skilled at socializing any new initiatives you're undertaking.
- With their experience, they provide an invaluable perspective. If you want to know if you are approaching this (DEI) work correctly, ERGs can be the perfect sounding board to understand how outreach might appear to different communities.
- They are incredible representatives, both in person and as an online presence. Those ERG members can attend recruiting events as panelists, presenters, or exhibitors.
- They can give credible context to what it's like to work in your company. Whether in-person or for online branding and marketing, they can share the day-in-the-life journeys at a company in a specific role in a way that speaks to your ideal candidates in the communities you're targeting. For example, they can allow potential candidates into their world and show what it's like to be your company's software developer, salesperson, marketing professional, or leader.
- They can serve as mentors for existing employees or new hires. One of the barriers to equity is the "pipeline of opportunities," which include mentorships, networking, and other advancement opportunities. ERG members can provide mentorship that facilitates growth, development, and advancement.

- They can be part of the team that solicits new hire referrals. They can build relationships and trust with the new hires, which helps with onboarding, strengthens workplace culture, and promotes company loyalty and longevity.
- They can assist in the interview process through strategy and interview ideas or by becoming a panel member (if you have interview panels).
- They provide fresh ideas and perspectives and allow the recruiting team to view outreach through the lens of the communities they're hoping to engage.
- Fully developed, integrated, and supported ERGs fortify you with authenticity. They show the world that you are "walking the walk" when conversations arise around diversity, equity, and inclusion. This is especially important during times of social unrest like we've recently experienced.

ERGs are amazing, but there are two things to highlight and clarify.

1. They must be vetted and able to showcase commitment to diversity and inclusion and the organization in general.

Additionally, you want them to be able to tell the story about how a person can start and grow their career with your organization because they will be those examples.

2. There is a massive difference between leveraging ERGs and ERG members and using employees from diverse communities to address diversity matters.

The vital distinction is this:

ERGs are voluntary. They have signed up to contribute more, address certain issues, and represent specific communities/identities.

But you should never assume employees from diverse communities are open to assisting in DEI matters or becoming community representatives.

That adds extra work outside of their job description, adds emotional labor of explaining specific social issues or perspectives, and it could be microaggressive, adding trauma to their daily experience.

Since ERGs have become more popular and adopted in the last few years, it was essential to include this part of the conversation around ERGs and how you would leverage them in your diversity recruiting efforts. By tapping into this deep well of talent, perspective, and experience, you'll be in a position to unlock a new world of opportunity.

To maximize all the components of your framework, it is important to ensure that you allow room and flexibility for collaborative learning, failure, and mistakes.

No one has all the answers and it will take some trial and error. Just be sure to learn from the mistakes, document, and share the wins and failures to bring the whole organization along on the journey.

There is no final destination on the DEI journey.

CHAPTER SEVEN

DIVERSITY STEERING COMMITTEE

What A Diversity Steering Committee Might Look Like

Determine the Stakeholders

Engage your CEO and other organizational leaders at the top of the organization. Then, seek passionate, like-minded coworkers who are willing to make their opinions known and defend a cause they support. Your DEI Steering Committee should consist of a broad group of individuals from various divisions across the business.

Steering Committee

The steering committee has overarching responsibility for the broad DEI strategy and has leaders from across the company with different backgrounds and different functional areas of responsibility.

The steering committee (or working group or whatever you call it in your organization) is essential to the framework that you're building. As noted earlier, this group should consist of different individuals across the organization. More importantly, you want to create some flexibility within the framework that you've created so that there is an opportunity to bring in fresh ideas and do different things.

You want the steering committee to be able to collect the best practices and share those across the company. The people who might be on this steering committee include:

- your executive leadership team
- your head of diversity and inclusion
- your head of talent acquisition
- the people who are representing employee resource group leadership
- the learning and development leadership
- the early-in-career recruiting leader
- HR and business leaders
- and a range of other people who have the authority to allocate budget and resources

This group collectively shares ideas that are going to champion change in the management, governance, and standardization across your company.

Understand where you're facing challenges right now:

Assess the diversity, equity, and inclusion issues your company faces before forming a diversity steering committee. For instance, it's possible your business benefits from employee recommendations.

Although they frequently have advantages, referrals can also result in a homogenous workforce and deter diverse candidates. Knowing the difficulties up front might help your diversity council have a defined objective.

Your DEI steering committee will leverage the framework to prioritize company-wide resource and funding decisions. I mentioned this previously, but it is worth repeating here. Having a framework provides the answers to why the company is choosing to prioritize one activity or engaging with an organization, conference, school, or event over others.

Your well-meaning employees and leaders will present many creative options for who, where, and how the organization should proceed with diversity recruiting efforts. If you reject their ideas, you risk creating disappointment and hostility if you don't have any criteria for how the decisions were made.

Go all in, but take baby steps. There will be many opportunities to do more, but to be successful, you've got to take this as a step-by-step approach.

If you already have a successful DEI program, think about how your steering committee will enhance those efforts.

The following are some recommendations to remember:

- Define the responsibilities and roles of the diversity steering committee members
- Choose partners for key efforts
- Create an accurate picture
- Determine expectations
- Establish meeting formats
- Follow up on and share progress
- Decide how to bring in new committee members
- Assign resources

Your diversity and inclusion efforts need to be employee engaged. However, without executive support (including assigning resources), it will be difficult to achieve your objectives.

In other words, when DEI is a priority at the leadership level, it will ensure that you have the necessary infrastructure—and budget—to fulfill your promises of diversity, equity, and inclusion in the workplace.

By establishing a diversity and inclusion steering committee, you give employees a way to participate directly in diversity and inclusion efforts.

CHAPTER EIGHT

DIVERSITY SOURCING

Where Is The Talent?

In this chapter, I'll talk a little bit about some of the key components of diversity sourcing. I want you to be able to update your approach to diversity sourcing, not with a bunch of amazing Boolean search strings, but just in connecting with more people and building more relationships.

In one of his pieces of training, Eddie Pate says, "We want you to be able to start and continue your journey of being an inclusive leader and being a better human." As your team begins or continues the effort to attract and hire a more diverse workforce, it is important to remember that there is no one-size-fits-all solution.

Before I go into ways to freshen up your sourcing efforts, I want to share a list of ten areas that will help you guide your overall diversity recruiting journey.

1. Ensure that your efforts to attract and hire candidates are genuine, honest, and transparent. Candidates will quickly be able to recognize when a company is just paying lip service to its diversity recruiting efforts.
2. Be cautious of generating buzzword-filled glossy ads and marketing content with all the perfect people in your stock photo glossy marketing material.

3. Just be real, use real people, and ensure that you are showing your true and authentic workplace. Candidates aren't looking for a perfect company. They are looking for real people with real talk.

4. There is no substitute for treating every candidate with dignity and respect. If you are attending a hiring event, give every candidate a fair chance and treat them the way you would expect to be treated.

5. Don't leave your recruitment to chance or "post and pray." Be intentional and deliberate about finding, engaging, and building trust with every candidate. To make progress in any community, they need to know, like, and trust you and your company.

6. Expand your internal employee referral programs to include people in your ERG and others who may not be in your majority population. People refer others who are like themselves, so broaden the referral network.

7. Take bias seriously and work to reduce and recognize your own bias and the bias of your interview teams and hiring managers.

8. Avoid the practice of hiding candidate information on the resume like names, schools, location, education, and other items that may give insight into a candidate's background or identity. I know that this contradicts the current practices implemented by many organizations.

9. Give your recruiters time to source and screen a truly diverse slate of candidates for every role. In order to do this, you have to slow down and provide your teams with the time and resources to find great diverse candidates who most likely are not applying to your roles.

10. Measure the diversity of your pipeline at several stages in the hiring process and use the data to drive actions and behaviors for your hiring efforts. Where are candidates falling out of the process and what are the demographics of those candidates?

Diversity Sourcing

Have you ever been stuck in your sourcing effort, and you just feel like, "I'm just not finding more people … I've already exhausted the candidate pool?"

While it may feel that way, we both know that's not the case.

Be strategic

One of the things we need to do as sourcing and recruiting professionals is to get more strategic, have more patience, and really put our hearts and our heads into the work we do in finding diverse talent.

We've got to be intentional, and we've got to be deliberate about it, because it's not going to happen by accident. Why do I say that? Because you need to be able to think like the candidates that you're trying to find and have the ability to relate to them. So, first and foremost, be more strategic and start with the end in mind. What are you trying to accomplish?

Then, go about building relationships. When I talk about building relationships, that doesn't mean you reach out to a candidate and say, "I've got a job." Certainly, that's part of the recruiting process, but you've got to start way before by getting to know those people that you're trying to reach out to because you don't have any credibility in this tough market.

It's a challenge when you're trying to recruit the same person that ten other people are trying to recruit, so you want to take what I call a multi-touch approach. Start by engaging the talent at your local level, if you're going to be involved with any organizations that are out there.

Secondly, you will need to be able to engage at the regional level, at the national level, and in some cases, at an international level, because multinational organizations have people working all over the world. *Remember, it's not about you. It's about what's in it for the candidate that matters to them.*

So, this is where it starts … it's the beginning. Be strategic, be intentional, be deliberate, and put yourselves in the shoes of those candidates and get that help.

You don't always have to have the recruiter pitch, but focus on adding value. Because in this market, people are looking for things that add value to their lives and make their lives better.

Be collaborative

The other thing you want to do is not try to do this in a vacuum. You can't do this work alone. A lot of the work and efforts rest on the shoulders of recruiters. Everyone thinks, oh, my recruiter is going to get me everything I need.

Well, that's not really true. You need help, so get partners, your hiring teams, your interview teams, and your workplace involved, because the more people that you have reaching out and connecting and building relationships, the better your pipeline and the better you're going to engage with those communities.

Do more to make connections. This doesn't mean that you have to be the one that personally makes the connection, because as the sourcer or the recruiter, if you get six other people to partner with you and do outreach, you've just 6x'd your ability to reach candidates.

Be prepared to slow down

Now, what I'm going to say next is counterintuitive to anything that we do as recruiters. You have to slow down to speed up. Don't always go with the first best candidate.

For example, if you're an amazing sourcer, then you can already write a Boolean search string, or you already have a tool that you're going to use that will zero in on the exact profile you're looking for.

Therefore, take a moment to slow down and go broader to find more communities and engage more people. That will place you in a pool of more diverse candidates. It may not result in finding the exact profile that you were looking for right off the bat.

Are your sourcing channels serving you or are they holding you back when it comes to finding diverse talent?

If I haven't mentioned this before, then I will now. We are creatures of habit. We are going to go to the channels that we know we've had success in. We're going to go to the same schools, we're going to engage with the same associations, we're going to recruit from the same companies, and we're going to use the same search strings.

In fact, we will, without a doubt, share those search strings with other people. The goal is for us to expand where we're looking, which means we've got to do something different to identify communities, organizations, and places where talent might reside where we wouldn't know to look.

The goal is to expand the pools that we're looking in. I always say, 'fish in the pools where they are and look at diversity more broadly,' especially when you're thinking globally. Look more broadly in places you wouldn't otherwise know to look in as a great recruiter.

Search for competitors that have affinity groups. Build your search results and build on those results because that will allow you to spring-board your efforts.

Too often, we find ourselves repeating one search only because it turned out to be an amazing search. We find information, but we also find information that we don't necessarily care for.

I'm telling you to look at that information and continue to build on the little pieces of data that you find that will lead you to a broader pool of candidates. That mindset change alone is going to allow us to find more great talent that we wouldn't otherwise see.

The bottom line is that there isn't a pipeline problem. Instead, we have a problem with the time spent on identifying people who might not otherwise show up in your specific search. Do something different every day. Are you going to those places where diverse communities exist, and are you building on your search results?

Take the time to really broaden your search and try something different. Don't let your search strings hold you back, go beyond your search strings. You can do these things regardless of where you sit on the planet and what region you're in.

You could take the same concept and you can be able to apply those and have an impact on your channels and your pipeline. So the point here is, nothing changes if nothing changes. If you don't change the behavior and do something different every day, then nothing's really going to change.

Take that extra time, slow down, and expand those areas that you're looking in.

What's your approach?

The next thing that you want to be able to do is to think about your approach and your methodology. How do you go about starting the recruiting process?

Review where you're actually looking for talent. Are the places you're going bogging you down, or are they serving you well and letting you find the people that you need?

Obviously, we're not doing a great job of this, because everyone's trying to diversify their workforce, and everyone's still struggling to get this done. But identify those communities, organizations, associations, groups, and networks where the people you're looking for are hanging out, and you will have success.

You can do a quick search: put in a keyword or demographic term, or just put those terms in and maybe a skill set or job title, and you're going to be able to expand who you're looking for.

Site search every day

Make sure that your site searching for something every day. If you don't know what I mean by site searching, it's using the "site" command to look at the information on a particular website.

Site searching tells a search engine that you want to search an entire site for keyword terms. For example, if you were to site search LinkedIn, you'd enter the following in your search bar:

- site:linkedin.com "diverse engineer"

TIP: *Search communities that your demographic participates in, because some great talent might not even have a LinkedIn account, but they might be on Instagram, Facebook, etc.*

You'd be surprised at the information that you can find by site search-ing some of the common sites, social media sites, or company sites that you're trying to find talent within.

So that's why I always say to do a site search every day.

That's a critical part of improving where you're finding talent.

Do something different every day

Don't just do the same thing ... try something different. It doesn't cost you anything to try something in a search.

It costs you nothing to pick up an article, watch your favorite reality TV show or documentary and look for people. Eventually, you will find leads and the breadcrumbs that may lead you to the talent that you're look-ing for.

And you're not specifically looking for a particular individual.

You're looking for organizations that will get you to more people who are in the community. We get trapped in looking for a specific title, but we don't find the organization or the community we need to find to get there.

What I know from experience is that people hang out with people who are like them. Once you get to that point where you're looking for the com-munity, and not the individual, it'll be a game changer.

Build on your results

Build on the results that you've already accomplished or that you've already found. Learn:

- what they do
- how they write
- how they communicate
- how they describe their work
- about their accomplishments

... and then use those things that you've learned in your sourcing approach and add those to your search strings and add those to the places that you look at.

What I'm really saying here is fish in a larger pool.

So give the pool more width and depth so that you are in a position to look at more people. Look for more and different skills, and look at the rewards and accomplishments people have had and use those terms in your searches.

Military Recruiting

Every company should think about bolstering their teams with veterans because they can provide significant benefits to any organization.

When hiring veterans, keep the following in mind:

1. Start simple by becoming a learner about the veteran community

   When employers and employees have a basic awareness of the principles, structure, policies, and expectations of the military, it creates stronger working relationships.

   If you already have veteran employees, using them in the recruiting process can be highly beneficial for understanding and connecting with veteran prospects. This is especially true if you want to recruit close to a military base where there will be more service members around than usual.

2. Understand the transferrable skills that veterans bring to the table

   The following are just some of the skills that veterans have which will prove helpful in your workforce.

   Leadership - Veterans understand that behavior is the key to effective leadership because they understand that it's important to lead by example.

Adaptability - It is said that the modern battlefield is unpredictable, complex, and ambiguous. Within tight quarters, today's veterans had to learn how to deliver aid, fight, and train foreign armies. Today's world is similar in that the environment can be unpredictable.

Decisiveness - Veterans are accustomed to making choices and accepting responsibility for the results if they are unfavorable. If everything goes well, they give the team credit, knowing that it will build trust.

3. Get the message right when reaching out to veterans

Creating a strong job description is an essential skill when attempting to hire veterans. Specifically, you may need to modify your existing job description to appeal to veterans. This is vital if the position is particularly applicable to a candidate with military experience.

Veterans will be able to see how their abilities and experience are pertinent and transferable to the role if your job description clearly outlines duties, in language that is clear and highlights common skills.

For instance, you might emphasize in your job description that you're looking for people with leadership or problem-solving skills, communication skills, flexibility to adapt to change, experience dealing with a variety of people, or technical skills.

Disability Recruiting

By actively seeking out individuals with disabilities you may create a workforce that is more diverse and attract a larger talent pool. The aim is to strengthen your team with the best talent. It's a challenging task given the continued labor shortages and the tight job market.

The fact is, by not hiring people with disabilities, you could be passing up on very competent candidates. The unemployment rate for those with disabilities is often significantly higher than the rate for those without disabilities.

You might unintentionally dissuade job applicants with disabilities from applying in the first place if you don't focus on creating inclusive job advertisements. Pay attention to your words, the recruiting procedures you follow (e.g., do you offer support?), and the job's requirements.

How can you improve your hiring procedures to attract people with disabilities?

1. Add marketing messages that are welcoming

For example, something like "we strongly encourage applicants with all abilities, disabilities, and backgrounds to apply. We don't practice disability discrimination."

2. Encourage current employees with disabilities to help with messaging

Ask employees with disabilities to share their experiences, and then publish those accounts on your organization's websites, brochures, social media pages, newsletters, and other channels that are used to reach a wide audience such as distribution lists for program outreach and application deadlines, including social media and print outlets for people with disabilities.

3. Connect with regional, national, and local organizations

To attract and accommodate individuals with disabilities it is crucial to establish relationships at organizations run by and partnered with persons with disabilities.

Some common resources of information and assistance include:

- university disability services offices
- local independent living centers
- rehabilitation programs
- adaptive recreation programs
- parent organizations
- special education departments or schools
- disability rights organizations and support groups

4. Offer scholarships

One of the most effective methods for encouraging underrepresented groups to participate is financial aid. Offer scholarships focused on people with disabilities specifically.

Make sure to also provide broader fellowships and scholarships to a variety of individuals.

5. Provide accommodations

Incorporating a "disability accommodation" line item into every project and administrative budget is the most reliable way to guarantee that resources are available when needed (1–3 percent of program costs is typically adequate).

Additionally, have outreach applications and materials prepared (or know where to find them) in accessible forms. If applicants with disabilities are aware of an organization's dedication to promoting inclusive participation, they could be more inclined to apply.

Engage Umbrella Organizations

One of the tips that I give people who are trying to diversify is to engage these umbrella organizations.

Here's what I mean by umbrella organizations. There are organizations that have a broad demographic membership. A lot of times we try to narrow down to a specific demographic, and there's nothing wrong with that.

That's certainly one of the approaches to use when searching for a specific demographic. If you're looking for women, for African Americans, for Latinx or if you're looking for people with a disability, then you can look at those organizations that serve those demographics.

But there's a group of organizations that I call "umbrella organizations." These organizations have all demographics and all the genders. For instance, organizations that serve LGBTQIA+ individuals have men and women and all kinds of different demographics, and that's a rich source for talent.

And that gives you a great opportunity to diversify. Organizations that work with people with disabilities: There is no discrimination in having a disability, because everyone in the group has a disability. The disabled community is the one group that anyone could become a member of at any point in their life, whether psychological or physical, so keep that in mind.

Veteran organizations: There are all kinds of people in the veteran organizations; you have people that are currently on active duty who are getting off and coming back, veterans. You have people who were veterans ten years ago, because they got out of the military. You have people who are not military and who are part of the veterans' organizations. So that's a big umbrella organization: men, women, almost every demographic you can imagine. And here's the one that we always miss for some reason, the alumni associations from schools. It might be an HBCU, or an Indigenous people-serving institution. It could be a women's school, or it could be a trade school. It could be a two-year college. The alumni have graduated, and now they're working somewhere. They've got skills, so look for those alumni in those organizations.

There are numerous places available to find alumni. People are proud of where they went to school, and they post it on their LinkedIn and their Facebook. They tweet about it on Twitter, and they join organizations from their school.

An available resource that people tend not to go to as quickly or as often would be boards. Is someone a member of a board? You can put all kinds of demographic terms with "board and member of," "serves on this board," or "a member of a council or a member of a committee." Those are other big umbrella organizations that typically have all kinds of demographics and professionals.

Then, look at things like your chamber of commerce. In the National Minority Supplier Development Council (NMSDC), you've got all kinds of companies. You have lots of different members, and you also have corporate members who have supplier diversity programs who are also engaged. You can even get companies to target, and you can find people to build relationships with to connect with the communities you're trying to connect with.

I talked about alumni, but the National Association for Colleges and Employers (NACE) is another example of a place where you could find alumni who have a connection to all these colleges, universities, and employers.

You can expand your search, expand where you're looking, and just improve the channels.

Early-in-Career and College Recruiting

This book is primarily focused on giving you the tools, processes, and strategies to build a comprehensive diversity recruiting strategy. It's important for me to call out some of the unique components of building an early-in-career college recruiting strategy that will enhance your diversity recruiting efforts.

One of the things that's critical when you're doing your college recruiting strategy is to start with the mindset of a multi-year strategy. Meaning, you need to think about twelve months ahead of the time that you want to make your first college hire and it could be twelve to eighteen months, if you're hiring full-time candidates out of a college program.

The earlier you start with your college recruiting efforts, the better. Some of the important things in your college and early-in-career recruiting efforts include:

1. Making sure that you are clear on the values that you hire for because most of the early-in-career people will not have the

experience and or the skills that you're looking for. So, this means you will be hiring more on potential and values.

2. At times, you will have a hard time getting your interviewers to adjust their mindset when it comes to hiring early-in-career talent for the reason that most people aren't doing that kind of hiring and interviewing.

3. It would help if you also considered giving something back to the candidates. College recruiting is a different animal than experienced-hire recruiting so you want to make sure that your company brand stands out. It's important to the college students or the early-in-career students coming out of trade schools or some certification program to know that your company values inclusion and diversity.

4. It should be easy for the individuals to determine if you're being genuine and authentic. The feeling shared between the two parties shouldn't feel as though you are simply trying to hire people. Instead, they should have a sense that you're hiring people who can start and grow their career in your organization. Authenticity is important and critical.

5. You also want to be able to evaluate your selection criteria; in some cases, you will have to upgrade your selection criteria.

Business Has Changed

For many years premier schools and GPAs were absolute requirements. That's not really the requirement if you're going to start to expand and broaden the pool of talent that you're bringing in; you're going to want to revisit what your criteria for selection and hiring might be.

GPA may not be that critical therefore going to a top-ten school may not be that critical; you'll have to make those decisions.

Create Opportunities For Engagement

Consider creating opportunities for students to learn collaboratively about what you're looking for, in a job or at your company. So, start thinking; the earlier you can engage with early-in-career students, the better.

Have a multi-year strategy and be thinking one, two, three, four, or even five years out, for when you want to get the candidates, and think in twelve-month increments. (But that twelve-month increment has to be before you're trying to make your first hire.)

And then, you want to build your on-campus strategy. You also want to have a virtual-campus strategy. For example, during the pandemic, many schools did not have in-person classes. They were online. How are you going to reach those students? How are you going to assess them? How are you going to get them to recognize your brand?

Create A Strategy

Make sure that you build an organization strategy and an event strategy that includes both in person as well as virtual, and that can be done through virtual career fairs, virtual fireside chats, conversations, or information sessions that you might have with leaders in your company.

Train your students on how to interview with your company. Train your interviewers on how to assess early-in-career talent, and ensure that they go through inclusive interviewer training resulting in a full understanding of how to interact with students.

Use your ERGs if you have them, or use people who are new to the company and who are early-in-career to relate to those candidates. Check out the various clubs and organizations on campus. Get closer to the career services organization because a number of students are going to go to career services for insight and most importantly, to build relationships with the faculty and the professors because they know who the best students are.

Faculty members and professors know which students are struggling and they know how to relate to those students on the course material as well as being an advisor to those students on jobs that they might want to consider.

Use Social Media

Do you have a social media presence? If not, this would be the time to start because your presence will matter.

A lot of up-and-coming early-in-career students are on social media. If you look at Gen Z now, they're digitally and technically savvy. They've always had access to technology, so make sure your company is seen as a company that knows how to communicate through various social channels.

Some of the things that you can do if you really want to have an impact are to focus on helping shape the curriculum that would lead people to get jobs in your organizations and be able to engage the students, build those relationships, and connect with all student organizations on the campuses there.

Engage with trade schools if you're looking for people who have to touch the equipment and need a special skills trade. Spend time getting to know those students early in the process and let them know, like, and trust your company.

Engagement Ideas

Maybe you're going to do things like provide scholarships. Maybe you'll do things like have campus ambassadors, who go to those schools and go through your internship programs. Maybe they go through a work-study program that you have.

Either way, the goal is to help students learn about your company and be in a position to make a decision, putting your company at the top of their minds when it comes time for them to select what job they're going to. Nearly all fraternities, sororities, and diversity organizations have student chapters. Those student chapters will give you access to a variety of students…some may even be engineering students.

Maybe you're looking at the National Society for Black Engineers, the Society for Hispanic Professional Engineers, the National Women MBA association, or Reaching Out MBA, which is the LGBTQ community MBA program.

All of those students are going to be at some campus somewhere and it may be a Tier One campus, it may be a Tier Two, or it may be a Tier Three. The tiering on the campuses should be related to the tiering that you defined for your company's diversity organizations: Tier One, Tier Two, and Tier Three.

As a reminder, a Tier One organization or school is one that has all the talent or most of the talent you want to hire across multiple business divisions. A Tier Two may be a school that is specifically focused on science and technology or engineering, finance, or human resources. Tier Three represents the schools that may be the alma maters for a number of people in your company. Unfortunately, they're just not going to get company-wide resources.

Those are a few things that you want to be able to consider as part of your early-in-career and college recruiting hiring efforts, which fits right into the strategy for your diversity recruiting efforts.

To summarize:

- You want to be able to take a multi-year approach
- Get to the students early
- Engage those students at a minimum of twelve months out because you are going to be recruiting in the year prior to when you want to have that student join your organization

Do things like:

- internships
- work-study programs
- scholarships
- information sessions that talk about your company, the different jobs, and the roles that students gravitate toward
- practice interviews (mock interviews) that help students know how to interview for your company (this will help you get a jumpstart on your competition as you are making early-in-career hires)
- getting more digital with your workforce and your workplace

Also, consider being able to:

- use technology for video interviews
- give technology assessments or competency assessments, or any of those things (ensure that these practices are vetted so that you don't inadvertently cause an adverse impact on your early-in-career hiring efforts)

The good thing about college recruiting is that colleges are all listed. You know the demographics, you know the locations, you know when school starts, etc. By putting together a strategy that allows you to go to selective colleges you've identified based on your company's needs and engaging those students, you will be able to be more targeted in your diversity recruiting efforts with early-in-career, college, and skilled-trade students.

Executive Recruiting

One of the most impactful things you can do with your diversity recruiting strategy is to ensure that you have built a plan for your executive leadership recruiting.

By hiring more diversity at the executive level in the company, you put yourself in a position to change the entire organization and the company's culture and solve for more extensive business problems.

Some of the things you want to consider with executive leadership recruiting include getting to know the talent. Executive recruiting will be different from your "every day experienced" recruiting, as well as your early-in-career recruiting.

Executive recruiting may take two, three, four, or five years to hire the right leader, because you are looking at what business problems they will help solve, or what markets this person is moving you into? What are they going to solve? What are they going to fix? Do you have the leadership that you need to take the company from where it is today to where it needs to go?

Some of the things that you want to consider when you're looking at hiring executives is to make sure that you're including a diverse slate of candidates in your executive search process.

For example, suppose you've got an internal executive recruiting team. In that case, you may want to encourage them (the hiring manager and your executive team) to have a slate of diverse talent that includes women, people of color, and other marginalized communities, who are different from the existing executive leadership team.

Things To Consider In Executive Search.

First, ask yourself, "Does this role need to exist?" And if the answer is yes, it does need to exist, then ask yourself, "But does it need to exist in the way that it's always been done?"

Or are you looking for something different? If it's a new role, then you want to craft the role, and as the head of talent, you want to have a hand in crafting what that role is supposed to do. What's this person supposed to accomplish?

And what values, skills, and competencies do you need for that role? One of the things that you're going to have to consider is your culture. Does your culture have a fixed mindset or a growth mindset? That's going to determine the kind of person you're going to hire.

A fixed mindset is about maintaining business as usual and protecting what you already have. However, a growth mindset is about expanding into new markets, developing new products and services, and innovating beyond your current products and services.

Internal Talent

Internal talent should also be considered. Do you have internal talent that could be on the succession plan, and could move into a role like this or a similar role? Or do you have to go out to the market and find talent for that role? For instance, do you have to go to competitors?

Do you have to look in the industry and find not the "number one person doing the job" but the "number two person"? Or can you find someone with similar skills, presently in a role that requires similar competencies but the name may not be the exact title you're looking for?

Values

Ensure that you are looking closely at your value set. What values are you looking for in bringing that leader on because every leader that you hire is going to impact your company's culture and the direction of the company.

What To Look For

An important piece of this is understanding the must-haves for the role and not necessarily all the nice-to-haves. You are looking for leaders who are curious, who build relationships, who know how to influence, and who empower others to do their best work.

You want someone who understands the process of setting boundaries and knows how to reset, renew, and restart business initiatives that may go wrong. You're looking for things they've done in the past, things they have been successful at, and things they are most proud of.

What were the duties that they did? How have they measured success? Do they have the business acumen, and can they look at profitability? Can they look at your revenue? Can they look at the cost? Can they look at performance and building high-performing teams? Pay attention to all of those details in your executive recruiting process.

Diverse Talent ... Building Bridges

Now, how are you going to get diverse talent?

Executives will not apply to your job, so your internal teams will need to do research.

They're going to need to

- target companies
- target industries
- target specific talent
- find organizations and start to build those relationships with the members

Keep in mind that relationship building doesn't happen overnight. It sometimes starts years before, and so you want to start to put yourself in a position to get your existing leaders or your board members to build relationships with people in diverse recruiting organizations, and in various organizations.

This means when your internal recruiting team reaches out, the talent will already know, like, and trust the person. More importantly, the talent they seek will already know, like, and trust your company.

What Are Executives Looking For?

Executives want to do work that allows them to make a big impact. You want to understand, what their dominant "buying" motive is. What are the things that they're looking for? Many of the things they want to look for will give them impact. They certainly want more scope and responsibility.

They certainly want to make sure that they're compensated fairly. And so, as you're thinking about your executive recruiting work, you really want to put the energy into taking your time.

Sometimes you have to "go slower to go faster," by making sure that you give your recruiting team the time to find the talent, engage the talent, and build relationships with the talent.

Use Inclusive Language

Once you start to get a job description make sure the language in that job description or that position description is inclusive. Often, women and underrepresented talent will opt out of a job because they don't believe they're qualified for the role.

So, create an inclusive marketing job description or position description that the talent will believe to be interesting.

Ask Good Questions

An interview guide will be a great resource for executives on the interview team and will ensure that they are not asking random questions. Instead, you want them to ask specific questions that go to the specific values, competencies, and skills you want to evaluate the candidate on and to make sure they're well trained and they understand how to conduct an interview.

Every person in that interview process is going to be selling the candidate as well as evaluating the candidate, but they need to sell the candidate on your leadership team.

They need to sell the candidate on your culture, their team, the organization, and where the organization is going. Ensure that your teams understand how to sell as part of any executive leadership recruiting effort.

What Does It Take To Succeed In The Role?

What is the priority of this role?

What are the reporting relationships? What impact do you expect this role to have on the short-term, mid-term, and long-term business? And what leadership will this new hire bring to the table that will allow your company to move forward?

Try working with your board to have a holistic strategic talent acquisition focus.

My good friend, Chris Bell, talks about strategic talent often.

Seek to answer questions such as:

- What will this role do?
- What are the strengths, weaknesses, threats, and opportunities that this role will allow us to address?

Building confidence in your candidate is another part of your executive leadership recruiting.

Sometimes you're going to need to prepare that candidate for their interview. You will need to coach them on some of the important things, how work gets done, and how decisions are made in your organization.

Your Hiring Process

As you go through this process, you've got your long list, you've identified the market, you have a shortlist, and you have a diverse slate of candidates. It's important to also get a diverse set of interviewers. This can include the diversity of gender, ethnicity, functional background area, etc.

There is a need to have people who understand what's important in the business, what's important in the company, and how this role will impact that work so that your company moves forward to solve the problems that it's trying to solve.

Many pieces go into finding talent. First, you've got to research the talent, and you've got to find those target companies and expand those using a number of tools (we'll provide a list of tools that you can use).

But a big part of your executive leadership recruiting is to:

- Give your recruiters time.
- Ensure that you're casting a wider net to reach more people in specific communities.
- Include a diverse slate of talent as part of your intentional, holistic strategy for diversifying the workforce and, most importantly, diversifying the leadership team.

Inclusive Job Descriptions

Your job description should be inclusive. I know this gets covered a lot, but think about the language in your job description and where you are posting the job description. And what is your company branding around the job description?

You can use tools like Textio, Clovers (acquired TalVista), Gender Decoder, Ongig, etc. that you can use to simplify those job descriptions and make them gender-neutral and more appealing to a diverse candidate.

What's your company's brand?

One of the big ones, and this is not necessarily the recruiter, but this is something that you need to have input in, and that is your company brand?

Is it inclusive?

Are you known for being an inclusive company? Do you—or your brand—take a stand on big social issues, or are you and your company absent from the conversation? You can't just sit on the sidelines, because communities notice and they recognize your absence. Do something different to find what John Lewis discussed (finding "good" trouble).

Meaning researching current events and social topics and following the trail that leads to those marginalized communities, where their civil liberties are being impacted by something, and speaking out.

It might be a law that's coming through at the federal, local, or state level, but if you find the people who are marginalized, you're going to find the people in the communities that you're trying to recruit for and help your candidates know what to expect from your interviews. Things like this go a long way.

No longer are the days when candidates don't have options. You've got to sell the candidate, but you need to make sure that they're prepared. It's a waste of time to put all this time and effort into building relationships, and getting a candidate interested in your role, only to have them fail in your interview process.

The underlying cause could be one of two things. Either they have poor interviewers, or they just didn't understand what you were looking for in their answers to your interview questions.

Avoid Tokenism Practices.

I read something the other day; someone talked about being one of only two women in an organization. She was included in every interview and had to go to every recruiting event, so she didn't have time to do her day job because she was the token woman being showcased for diversity and inclusion.

I'm all for making sure that you reflect the diversity in your organization, but be thoughtful about how you bring others to the table and don't make them into your token person.

Recognize and mitigate your bias

The biggest issue is recognizing and adjusting for bias in your hiring process. Certainly, there's a lot of conversation about interview bias, mitigating bias, unconscious bias, and implicit bias in the interview process.

If you're human, you have bias. We all must check that bias, but I want to share how your goal of "hiring for culture fit" destroys your inclusion and diversity efforts. I've talked about this prior, yes. What I want to talk about, though, now is checking your sourcing channel bias. Do you lean toward one sourcing channel? And do you always go to that one sourcing channel or search for that one title or one skill set? Or are you expanding that title?

Make sure that you're expanding the titles and the places you're sourcing, and doing something different every day to find a broader pool of candidates. One of the things that I'm guilty of, and I think a lot of people are probably guilty of, is seeing a LinkedIn profile that's not built out, and ignoring that profile and just moving on because there's a minimal amount of information.

Keep in mind that sometimes that's done by design; that candidate does not want to be found. They might have a misspelling and/or they might have a poorly designed profile.

We have people on our team, who I would have never recruited because their LinkedIn profiles didn't say that they had ten years of recruiting experience. They had other things up there that were important to them. Fortunately, we've since changed that practice, but don't allow that bias to keep you from seeing a great candidate.

Expand more on titles by looking at the impact that people have had in their roles and the responsibilities that they've had because they may have accomplished many things in their roles.

I'll take a software developer, for example. They may never put the word "software developer" on their profile; they may call it something else. That role could be called something different depending on where you are in the world.

But the responsibilities of the job, the things they accomplish, and how they get their work done will make a difference. I tell everyone to define what diversity means in their organization and in their country, and in their region of the world, because that's important as well.

Understand where you are and what diversity is to understand where those communities exist, and how you can get to those communities without impacting any laws or privacy laws.

Clearly Define What You're Looking For

One of the things that I think is important is to make sure that you are defining what you want and what you're looking for. Many times we're thinking about sourcing and recruiting as this tactical thing. We're doing a lot of execution work, but I always say to put your heart and your head into recruiting.

This bears repeating … the diversity recruiting business requires a thinking, feeling, and caring mindset, and to be successful, you have to use your head and open your heart because that's what's going to get you connected to the communities you're trying to work with.

Be Intentional

Work backwards to meet the goal. Sometimes you hear that as "start with the end in mind." Know what you're looking for and what you're trying to accomplish.

I'm not telling you anything you don't already know, but get out there and build those relationships, using a multi-touch approach. So that means going to different places, meeting different communities, building relationships and getting to know those communities you're trying to connect with.

You can't just show up one time and expect those candidates to really love and care about you. It doesn't matter if you have a big brand. They don't necessarily know, especially in some of the diverse communities, what your company is about or what you're about as a person.

And I'll talk a bit about inclusivity in the brand. Sometimes you just have to go out, meet the candidates, and get to know that talent before you ever know about the opportunity.

Because, like people who purchase things, candidates want to work for companies that they know, they like, and they trust, so build those trusting relationships.

This is so important—you don't want to miss this.

When a company I worked for started its diversity efforts, it went to one of the big national events. Naturally, they expected to get a lot out of it. The candidates didn't know who they were, so they weren't that interested in speaking with them.

You have to take that first step and start to engage that talent. You may engage them locally, or regionally (meaning in the geographic region), or you might be engaging them nationally or internationally. Nevertheless, your brand is important and getting those candidates to know who you are and what you stand for is so critical to success.

Relationship Building Activities

There are some things you can do to help nurture relationships with diverse talent. For example, you can be a guide on how you do a diverse-a-thon.

Diverse-a-thons are sourcing events; they allow you to get more people involved in the sourcing and recruiting process and to find more of that talent. For the teams working virtually, you could still do diverse-a-thons. You don't have to be in the same room or in the same office to do that.

You can set up the diverse-a-thon, and make it online if you want to, but the main thing is to put the work in and do these diverse-a-thons on a regular basis because that's going to give you the ability to attract more talent.

One of the high-level things you want to do with the diverse-a-thon is to identify the role you will focus on and invite your hiring managers and other leaders to those diverse-a-thons.

Get your sourcing team members to join those diverse-a-thons. Gather recruiters, and coordinators … get anybody that you know to participate in that diverse-a-thon, because diversity and recruiting, is a team sport. It's not an individual thing.

Establish a process and communicate to everyone what the expectations are for that diverse-a-thon. Certainly, bring your laptops and be on your computers. Use the whiteboard (and you can do that electronically, or you could do that physically if you're with your team).

Search personal networks for your teammates. Search your hiring managers' networks and search for people who are in ERG and look at their networks.

A perfect example is LinkedIn. Look at:

- The first and second-level connections that some of your team-mates have on LinkedIn.
- The organizations that they belong to.
- The alumni associations that they belong to, and then build out that list for outreach.

And then start that outreach. And you can do that in a number of ways. If you have automation tools and people who will specifically do the out-reach for you, do you use them?

For example, have content on your LinkedIn profile that highlights your company's work and the focus on diversity and maybe even add it to your headline on LinkedIn.

Why?

Because that's going to cause the candidates to look at your profile right away. However, I don't always recommend on the initial outreach that you lead with it because the candidate will think, "Oh, they're just reaching out to me because I'm a diverse candidate."

You want to ensure that candidates don't feel like you're targeting them because of their identity or diverse background. Granted, you found them because you were intentional about sourcing and using a variety of channels and tools that would provide a diverse pool of candidates, but their identity was only part of the effort to engage the community in this situation.

It will help build more trust if you reach out to candidates in your target demographic with helpful information not just when you have a job opening. Try sending useful content, articles and information that might be of interest to them and provide them with tips and recommendations that would highlight what your company thinks is important to your business.

So, my advice is to update your profile with interesting information that's going to get more eyeballs on it than just one individual on LinkedIn.

This is not a tools book, but I wanted to include a few tools and a link to other downloadable resources. Below are a few tools that might be helpful as you consider diversity sourcing. I also recommend Jonathan Kidder's book *Top Talent Sourcing Tools for Recruiters,* available on Amazon.

Tools and Tactics

- Google Search Boolean (Natural Language)
- LinkedIn Advance Search – https://www.linkedin.com
- LinkedIn Recruiting Filters – https://www.linkedin.com/cap/dashboard/home
- CSE – Google Custom Search –https://www.linkedin.com/pulse/strategic-recruiter-custom-search-engines-chris-bell/
- hireEZ – https://hireez.com/
- TalVista (Acquired by Clovers)– https://www.talvista.com/
- SeekOut – https://seekout.io/
- Other tools can be found at The Search Authority – http://thesearchauthority.weebly.com/tools.html

Free Tools

Google

Google has a thing called "natural language search," which allows you to put in terms and look for people in a way that people may talk. This is going to help you surface things like bios, profiles, news articles, and/or any kind of awards recipients.

For example, if you put in "she is" and you put "software engineer," then that is going to pull up people where that content is. So, if someone's bio includes those terms, you're going to find that LinkedIn bio.

LinkedIn

And this is just the advanced search in the free version of LinkedIn, not necessarily LinkedIn Recruiter. There are lots of filters on LinkedIn that allow you to search for specific schools, names, locations, and titles. On the paid tool LinkedIn Recruiter, you can create filters that allow you to filter out.

For example, you may have a list of historically black colleges and universities (HBCUs) or Hispanic (HSI)/Latinx serving institutions or women's colleges, etc. You can filter (using Google or LinkedIn filters) specific schools and locations.

You can also do this in a bulk way using a Google Custom Search Engine. My friend, Chris Bell, built and wrote an article about the Google Custom Search Engine, including how to use it. There's lots of information out there, and there are some pre-built custom search engines you can use as well.

Paid Tools

hireEZ

There's a product called hireEZ which is an AI sourcing platform. It allows you to filter diverse talent, and you can set the AI to start looking for roles and finding people.

hireEZ is a great option to give you more lift with the volume of sourcing on the specific roles that you're looking for and the ability to filter on diverse talent.

TalVista

Part of the effort to get diverse talent more interested in your roles is to work on the job descriptions you have, making them more gender neutral and inclusive.

TalVista is a tool that gives you a score on the content of your writing and the content of those job descriptions. If you run your job ads through the TalVista platform, it will allow you to make your language and your content much more inclusive.

Seekout

Seekout is another, very powerful tool. Much like hireEZ, it will allow you to do automated searching and uses AI that will filter on diversity too.

TIP: *Visit the link below for an extensive list of diversity recruiting sources that can help you find the top diverse talent you need.*

https://codylhorton.com/thank-you/

PART V
STRATEGY AND MEASURING

"Things aren't always easy, but you just have to keep going and don't let the small stuff bog you down."
~ Stella Maeve

CHAPTER NINE

THREE-PHASE DIVERSITY STRATEGY

You often hear people talk about executing a three-year plan. Well, the amount of time it takes to get from one phase to the next might be different depending on your organization. This is because there are components in each phase that have to be put in place before you're ready to move to the next stage.

Some companies might do it in three months, three quarters, or three years, and some companies might take much longer. That's why I talk about a diversity hiring effort in phases rather than in a specific time frame. On the next page, you will see a graph explaining the entire framework.

3 Phase Plan Roadmap

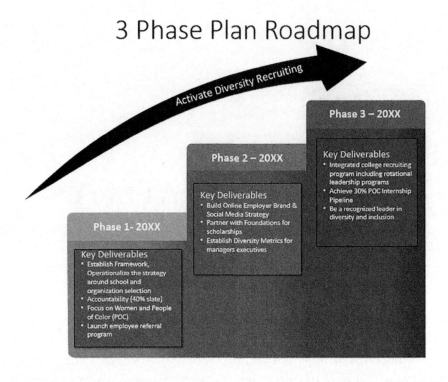

Build Your Foundation

You want to start by making sure you have a clear mission and vision. Create your mission and vision so that you are able to talk about why you're doing this and what you're going to do and what you're going to accomplish.

Establish High-level Goals For Diversity Recruiting Strategy.

Some of the things that might go into the high-level goals on that spread-sheet or on that slide could be:

- Increasing the representation of people of color, women, or other underrepresented groups to reflect the pool of available talent

- Building and strengthening partnerships with diverse communities, education institutions, alumni associations, and other professional organizations and associations
- Increasing accountability of the leaders to have diverse slates of talent for all hires or for hires at a specific level and above—at the director level or the manager level—you have to have a slate of diverse talent
- Providing training and development to 100% of the leaders or 80% of leaders and managers to foster diversity recruitment efforts and talent strategies
- Establishing a goal that says you want to become an employer of choice or a brand of choice where employees act as brand ambassadors and provide diverse referrals

Those are examples of high-level goals. Your goals are going to vary depending on the organization, but each organization is going to really assess what their organization needs and what their goals will be. Keep in mind that you must ensure that the goals are aligned from the top to the bottom of the organization.

There are internal things that you want to look at, like:

- Identifying the key stakeholders.
- Ensuring you've identified the right amount of training.
- Finding those champions in the company or in the divisions that you're going to support.
- Being able to work with the recruitment team for sourcing and recruiting strategies.
- Working with your talent management team to make sure that you've got talent management plans and efforts underway.
- Identifying or building ERGs. Those are employee resource groups, or business resource groups that can support carrying out your mission.
- Making sure that you've got employee engagement and that the employees are either asking for this or benefiting and participating.

- Doing a compensation review or a salary review as a part of your strategy to ensure that you've got equitable compensation and pay plans.
- Building a succession plan for developing or hiring the leaders who are going to take over in the future from the leaders who are currently in place.

Ensure that you engage the hiring managers, and you definitely want leader and executive C-level involvement. You want to ensure that you have diverse slates of talent, and that you're looking at promotion, retention, and attrition rates.

External things to pay attention to:

The external things that you want to pay attention to and habits as components of your strategy are:

- How are you going to work with local communities?
- How are you going to work with passive candidates?
- How are you going to deal with employee or ambassador referrals?
- How are you going to deal with new hire debriefs?

When you get a new hire, will you have time to go in and ask those new hires for referrals when you first hire them? That's when they're most likely to make good referrals.

You want to work with:

- Partner organizations
- Your target schools

Make sure you keep the target school list manageable. You may have pilot schools that aren't necessarily the target schools, but explore the opportunity to work with some of those different schools you may not have worked with for your early and career efforts.

Look at student clubs. You want to look and engage with professors who are influencers who also know who the best students are, and you want to be able to get student presentations and see how students communicate and whether they map to your company's core values, and the competency and the attributes that you're looking for in the company.

- Scholarships/programs/fellowships

You may have scholarships, programs, or fellowships, things that say, "Hey, we're trying to set up a company where people can start and grow their careers in the company."

You also want to look for people who were in the company before. (We call them boomerangs.) They may be people that left who were great and you want to get them back.

On the next page, you will find an overview of each potential phase.

Example

Phase One	Phase Two	Phase Three
Establish the framework	Building your employer brand	Integrate your college recruiting program with a rotational program
Operationalizing the strategy around schools, events, and organizations	Executing your social media strategy	Achieve previously established hiring metric
Building metrics and goals for accountability	Partnering with other organizations	*Perhaps a goal involved getting listed in a credible magazine as a leader in diversity and inclusion. Regardless goals should be met in Phase Three.
Focusing on more women and people of color and determining how to engage externally	Establishing more diversity metrics for hiring managers, recruiting teams, and executives	
Internal engagement and Launching Employee Referral Programs		

Here are two examples of what this layout may look like on paper.

Goal	Deliverable	Year 1 – 20XX	Year 2 – 20XX	Year 3 – 20XX
Increase sourcing and recruitment	Establish Tiered School and Diversity Organization Priorities	Identify Tier 1, 2, and 3 Schools - Q4 Identify 5-HBCUs/5-HSI – Q4 Identify Tier 1 diversity orgs- Q4 (This will include the LearnVest footprint)	Identify Executive sponsors - Q1 School Captains – Q1 Build school teams – Q1 Deepen relationships HBCU/HSI's - Q1 Deepen relationships w/ div orgs – Q1	Evaluation
	College Recruiting Planning RACI	Create college recruiting planning calendar for HO with RACI Model – Q3	Expand planning calendar to include HO and field –Q3	
	Summer Internship Program	Summer 20XX Internship Program Invite firm-wide participation – Q2 Execution and Framework – Q3 Survey interns and managers – Q4	Revise summer Internship Program based on feedback – Q2 Include additional functional areas- Q2	Achieve 30% POC Internship Pipeline - Q1 internship Intern class should be 30% POC
	MBA/Undergrad Camp			Design camp focused on diverse candidates – Q1
	Diversity Events Calendar for College and Experience Hiring	Consortium Graduate Study in Management Conference - Q2 ALPFA Conference – Q3 Develop Tier 1 diversity events calendar – Q4	Tier 1, 2 and 3 diversity events calendar – Q2	Tier 1, 2 and 3 diversity events calendar – Q2
	Experience hiring focus	Recruit and Interview at diversity conferences – Q3 Partner with ERGs – Q3 Post on diversity job sites – Q4	Build diversity sourcing and pipeline toolkit – Q1 Conduct research mapping of specific areas at competitor firms - Q2	
	Employee Referral Program	Implement the employee referral program – Q4	Announce the employee referral program thru CEO challenge July 2016 at our annual meeting – Q2 Launch and Implement employee referral program – Q2	

Goal	Deliverable	Year 1 – 20xx	Year 2 – 20xx	Year 3 – 20xx
Become an employer brand of choice	Employer Branding and Social Media Presence	Create Recruiting Content Assess and measure current Employer Brand through Linkedin, Glassdoor reviews, SEO Survey candidates and applicants and internal teams	Develop consistent look, feel and engagement effort across divisions Build Online Employer Brand Create Social Media Strategy	Recognition as a best place to work Such as • Diversity Inc
	Engage talent communities	Roll out pilot branded events at Conferences, meet ups by targeted location and on campus	Create improved use of video and interactive media to engage talent	
Build and strengthen partnerships	Engage Diversity Organizations	Multi-touch Approach - Local, Regional, National Prioritize sponsorships - Bronze, Silver, Gold etc. - Measure Corporate Social Responsibility Index with Diversity Communities	Partner with organizations Create academic scholarship for women and POCs Review scholarships and sponsorship levels	

As you can see, you'd have a goal and create some deliverables to help you achieve each goal. And then, you might have Phase One, Two, and Three. I've used Year One, Year Two, and Year Three in this case.

In the example, the goal is to increase sourcing and recruitment, and in order to do that, the deliverables are to establish a tiered school and diversity organization priorities list.

Notice the "College Recruiting Planning RACI," which means who:

- is Responsible
- is Accountable
- do you Collaborate with and
- do you have to Inform?

You may want to start or grow your summer intern program, or you may want to start a winter intern program … you could start many different things. You may want to have an MBA and undergrad campus recruiting initiative or include attendance at diversity events and publish a diversity event calendar for both college and experienced higher recruiting. As you're focusing on that higher-recruiting experience, be intentional. Then launch that employee referral.

Each deliverable gets more detailed as you go across the spreadsheet. In Year One, you're not going to do everything. We may say the goal is to increase sourcing and recruitment, and the deliverable is to establish a tiered school and diversity organization priorities.

You might decide to identify the Tier One, Two, and Three schools by the fourth quarter, or whenever you say. Or you might choose to identify five HBCUs and three Hispanic serving institutions by Q4, then identify Tier One diversity organizations by Q4. Those are examples of what to include.

In Year Two, you may extend this and do other things. In Year One, you established tiered schools and diversity organizations, so in Year Two, you might:

- identify additional executive sponsors by Q1

- have school captains build school teams
- deepen relationships at the HBCUs/HSIs
- deepen relationships with the diversity organizations

In Year Three, you'll evaluate, see where you need to make adjustments, and continue to evaluate. There is no such thing as a perfect plan, no exact timeline, or a final delivery date for success. The three-phase plan is just an example. Your plan may have many more steps and take much longer, but the key is to document your plan and treat it like a living document. Give yourself the grace to iterate on your plan and adjust it as you learn more.

CHAPTER TEN

WHAT GETS MEASURED?

In this chapter, I'll share the following:

- How to measure performance.
- How to measure your workforce.
- Where to look to get the right measurements.
- How to have the right scorecard to help you evaluate where you're going as a leader, as a business in the space.
- How hiring for "culture fit" has a negative impact on your inclusion and diversity efforts.

Some things that get measured can include:

- Brand engagement
- Pipeline
- Interviews
- Offers
- Hires
- Promotions
- Attrition
- Referrals
- Executives
- Suppliers

TIPS: *Don't just focus on the numbers ... understand the meanings behind each metric. What message are the numbers telling you? What issues do the numbers uncover? What behaviors are you trying to drive?*

What's Your Mindset?

To begin, the most important thing that will help is your mindset. It's important to be intentional about creating impactful results from the sourcer-recruiter relationship. I've always said that recruiting is a "head and HEART mindset." To succeed, you must use your head and open your heart!

Hiring is a team effort, and every person in the hiring process has a role to play ... candidates, sourcers, recruiters, coordinators, hiring managers, and interview teams all have a role to play. To be clear, I'll be talking about the kind of sourcer who finds and talks to candidates.

The sourcer-recruiter relationship impacts diversity recruiting and general success. Whether you have internal teams, contractors, or recruiting and sourcing teams as service partners, these practices will help you improve your impact through the sourcer-recruiter relationship.

It's A Partnership

I'll focus on the partnership between sourcing and recruiting, and how you can get the best results. If there is no partnership, you will have limited success with your diversity recruiting.

Define and clarify the roles of your sourcers and recruiters.

A sourcer's main job is to support recruiters in their sourcing efforts. Usually, the sourcer makes the initial outreach to the candidate. Recruiters manage the interviews, the internal process up to onboarding pre-work, the new hire's start, and the first ninety days.

Align your sourcers' and recruiters' goals and responsibilities.
Where do the sourcer and recruiter responsibilities start and end in your process, and how do you measure success?

Hire the right profile for sourcers and recruiters.
This is not a one-size-fits-all thing. Sourcers and recruiters have different internal motivations, and it shows in their results.

Clarify the "hand-off" process.
- Who owns the candidate?
- What are the rules of engagement?
- Credit the sourcer for candidates.
- Respect time for both
- Track jobs list
- Set a plan for sourcers
- Set clear goals, set expectations, and prioritize

Communication And Feedback Loop
Create a Service Level Agreement (SLA) Playbook; don't wing it. Build relationships, trust each other, collaborate, meet, record the intake, make each other look good, and solve problems together because you're in it together.

Have empathy for each other. Don't blame. Give credit and keep your eye on the goal.

Develop And Execute A Strategy
Maximize communication:

- Schedule regular check-ins
- Share the pipeline report
- Bring the sourcer into the intake whenever possible
- Regularly change and calibrate so that everyone is on the same page

Don't "follow your gut" because that can often lead to unconscious bias. Instead, leverage data to make informed decisions.

Track Time

Use metrics like sourcer submission to recruiter time, recruiter to HR time, and time to receive feedback. Time is a critical metric that applies to both the sourcer, the recruiter, and the interview process. Unfortunately, time is not on your side in a hyper-competitive market, so you want to use metrics.

Share Candidate Sentiment And Learning

Share data and use your ATS and CRM to track data like hiring demographics, source of hire, source of candidates, and pipeline.

Metrics And KPIs For The Sourcer:

- Submission to the recruiter to accept ratio
- When you submit candidates, did the recruiter accept them, or did they reject them?

  If the recruiter rejected a high number, you need to make an adjustment somewhere in your sourcing or something changed in the job that the recruiter hasn't communicated to you; it's back to that communication thing.

- Time to submission
- Recruiter satisfaction with the sourcing effort

  That's an important one because the recruiter is going to have a perception of how valuable that relationship is, and you want to ask them.

  Feedback is a gift; so sourcers need to know how satisfied that recruiter is and any kind of feedback on the candidates is information you want to include.

- Feedback checkpoint on candidate quality
  If you're getting poor feedback on all your candidates, there's an adjustment that you can make very quickly. But if you don't know about it, you can't make the adjustment.

Metrics And KPIs For The Recruiter:

Share feedback from the hiring manager with sourcer. Now for the recruiter, you want to be able to share feedback from the hiring manager with the sourcer. How often are you doing that?

Hiring manager satisfaction

Because the recruiter is interfacing with the hiring manager, satisfaction indicates how well you're doing. It's not just hiring; as a recruiter, you also want to measure the percentage of people in your interview loops.

100% Completion of Inclusive Interview Practices

As interviewers complete your inclusive interview training and use your inclusive interview practices, measure that information because that's going to get to the quality of the interviewers and their capability.

Interview Scorecard Completion

The recruiters should ensure an interview scorecard, and you want to look at the completion rate for the interview scorecard. Not that you just have a card to have it, but is everyone filling in the entire part of the scorecard so that you create consistency?

KPIs:

- Interview-to-hire ratio
- Number of hires

Candidate Experience Satisfaction

You also want to share candidate sentiment that comes from the sourcer when they're talking to people further up in the funnel. Candidates always tell them why they want to engage you or why they don't want to engage you, so they're going to be able to get data like:

- Is it your location?
- Is it your company brand?
- Is it the compensation?
- Time to submission to the hiring manager.
- Hiring manager submission to IV ratio.

These metrics are critical since they are items that can be tracked, discussed, and worked through to improve your process.

The sourcers will have the most current information that can be shared with the rest of the team. You also want to share data and use your ATS, your CRM, or the hiring demographics. Once someone is hired, use data like the source of hire to identify where your talent is coming from.

Show the source of the pipeline. You want to say, "Where are the buckets that this pipeline came from? What pools have we been looking in, and what talent are we finding in those pools?"

And we want to look for things that say, "This bucket of talent tends to decline to engage us." Those things will help you make decisions.

Shared Metrics

These are the metrics that link the recruiter and the sourcer at the hip.

Candidate experience satisfaction

This is a big one because the candidate is going to assess how well the entire process worked and if they got the job. It's one thing if they didn't get the job and another thing if they did. Recruiters, sourcers, and the whole interview team share this metric.

Time to submission to the hiring manager

That's a shared responsibility. I listed it for the recruiter, but the sourcer plays a major part in that effort.

Hiring manager submission to interview ratio

Sourcer is not a junior recruiter	Recruiter – not all recruiters are sourcers
Talk to candidates	Typically, don't have time to source
Research	Intake
Find candidates	First interview
Outreach and engage candidates	Process and account management
QIA screen Ask for referrals	Interview prep
Know market	Interview schedule
Understand competition	Debrief
Blueprint "want," "need," and "motivations" for a new role	Pre-close
Assess for role	Extend offer
Set expectations	Negotiate offer
14 – 21 days for initial QIA submittals to recruiter	Close
Leverage technology	6 weeks to interviews in process moving toward finalists
Use tools Automation tools, AI tools Measure response rates, open rates, engagement rates	8 weeks to hire (40-45 days)
	Hire
	Solicit referrals
	Pre onboard
	30-, 60-, 90-day check-in
	Internal systems and HR tools

How many of those submissions does the hiring manager say, "Yes, we want to go forward, and we want to interview that candidate"?

Let's make a tactical comparison of the recruiter and the sourcer roles:

Never Go Around The Recruiter

Never go around your recruiter as the sourcer unless they say, "Go around us and work directly with the hiring manager." You don't want your recruiter to be blindsided. If the recruiter feels that you consistently communicate with them, the recruiter will become a partner in the process because of the shared responsibility between the sourcer and the recruiter.

Always Offer To Help Your Recruiter

You'll build trust when you're available to help, and as a sourcer, you're in a better position to help the recruiter because you've already got those skills of interaction.

Tips:
For relationship building with candidates …

Sourcers:
Get to know the talent before you know about the opportunity, nurture campaigns, and value-added content.

Recruiters:
Stay in touch with the talent during and after the introduction, feedback, updates, and shop for other roles.

For intentional actions for success
- **Record intake** – sourcing teams hear what was discussed during the intake. It's best to include the sourcer in the role intake meeting.
- **Record screens** – the screener can focus on the conversation with the candidate, screener feedback and training.

- **Provide weekly reports** and meet to discuss specifics in detail.
- **Feedback loop** – from Interviewers, HM, recruiter and sourcer.
- **Give credit** to each other.
- **Use sourcers** as a specialist.
- **Use recruiters** as relationship and process management consultants.

For consistency
- Standardize interviews and phone screens
- Use phone screen scripts
- Use interview guides

Common Questions and Answers:
Question:
How important is a service level agreement to work together as a team?

Answer:
Very important to set clear and unambiguous rules. Create something that's going to give you the ability to measure stages in your process and give you feedback and influence, and information that would allow you to make a decision and the SLAs should be tied to the goal.

For example, if your hiring goal is to hire someone in the next sixty days, you want to back the process up and set the milestones in your SLA and the responsibilities in the SLA so that everyone can see if they're doing the things that they need to do. I suggest that you use that SLA as a living document; that SLA can change and it can change by role or by job family because not all jobs are created equally.

You can get key components in that SLA from the metric section, but as far as the process, the SLA is just an agreement up front on how you're going to work and what the results are.

Question:
How do I encourage the recruiter to see themselves as a partner in the hiring process?

Answer:
Build trust, share insight, share pipeline reports for funnels, ask them to get HMs to reach out to top talent when they won't respond to sourcers and recruiters, ensure that they always have enough information to be a trusted advisor to the client. Never go around them and blindside them. Always offer to help.

Question:
What is the best way to keep track of the data we collect to help us make better decisions?

Answer:
Use your ATS or CRM to track everything, report weekly and discuss the data and tell the story with the data.

Highlight trends, patterns, and learnings so that the recruiter can share this information with the hiring manager. Identify problems and troubleshoot together to find the root cause. (e.g., Offer declines: a root cause is comp, location, title, brand, etc.)

Use reporting from your HR system of record to measure:

- quality of hire
- performance over time
- tenure
- diversity
- promotion rates, etc.

This should be part of your broader talent strategy, and responsibility lies outside of the talent acquisition function but should be shared to better inform the sourcing and recruiting strategies.

Here are some commonly asked questions and answers. I encourage you to create your own list of questions and answers as part of your execution strategy.

Question:

How do I set boundaries as a sourcer without offending the recruiter or hiring manager?

Answer:

Start by setting expectations up front on the time it will take. Use the SLA, communicate often, ask questions, raise concerns, and share data. Be proactive and earn trust by being resourceful. Don't operate in a vacuum; research everything: the market, competitors, industry, etc. Make it your goal to help the recruiter look like a rockstar.

Question:

Should we build our own sourcing team?

Answer:

As a TA leader, I recommend that you budget enough money to hire and develop great recruiters. You should also budget funds to either build your sourcing team or outsource the sourcing efforts to expert sourcers. If you can't be sure that your sourcers will only do sourcing-related work, don't build the team and just outsource the sourcing.

Question:

The culture of a company is defined by the behaviors that are rewarded. What are some of the strategies that you've seen help to reward sourcers and recruiters for building a diverse pipeline?

Answer:

Sometimes it's a hiring reward. It's not paying for a quota, but if you put it in the goals that "X percentage of your hires should be in a range"—and I don't say put a specific percentage on it—have a range that says, "These roles have this addressable market," and we want to make sure that we're hiring either at market or above the market.

For example, the range could be 20 to 35 percent or whatever you want in a specific demographic because that's the addressable market for that role. Recruiters would get rewarded and a bonus for hitting their targets and hitting their goals across hiring.

CHAPTER ELEVEN

DEMOGRAPHIC AND DATA RESOURCES

In this chapter, I want to share some demographic resources and some data resources and tools that people can use to help create the data and a plan.

For example, if you say, "I want to hire 50 percent women in these engineering roles," but the population only produces 30 percent, you can make a realistic target as to what that goal should look like (e.g., a target range rather than a specific number).

In this example, you'd say, "I want to hire 25 to 28 percent of women for this role," which is a goal that's driven by the population data.

Demographic and Data Resources

U.S. Census
https://www.census.gov/quickfacts/fact/table/US/PST045218
The goal of the Census Bureau is to be the top source of accurate information about the country's population and economy. Their objective is to deliver the gathered data and services offered in the most timely, relevant, cost-effective, and high-quality manner possible.

U.S. Equal Employment Opportunity Commission - EEOC
https://www.eeoc.gov/statistics/employment/jobpatterns/eeo1/2018
The U.S. Equal Employment Opportunity Commission (EEOC) is in charge of enforcing federal laws that prohibit discrimination against job applicants and employees based on the following:

- Race
- Color
- Religion
- Sex (including pregnancy and conditions associated to it)
- Gender identity
- Sexual orientation
- National origin
- Age (40 or older)
- Disability
- Genetic information

All workplace activities, such as hiring, firing, promotions, harassment, training, pay, and benefits, are subject to the laws.

U.S. Bureau of Labor Statistics
https://www.bls.gov/home.htm
To aid in public and commercial decision-making, the Bureau of Labor Statistics collects data on the labor market, working conditions, price changes, and productivity in the US economy.

Department of Labor
https://www.dol.gov/
The Department of Labor's mission is to cultivate, promote, and develop the welfare of American wage earners, job seekers, and retirees; to improve working conditions; to expand employment options that are profitable; and to ensure rights and benefits associated with the workplace.

City-Data.com
City-Data.com

City-Data is a website that provides statistical information on cities across the U.S.

Equal Employment Opportunity EEOC Title VII
Title VII of the EEOC is an extension of the Commission on Civil Rights. Its purpose is to prevent discrimination in federally assisted programs. The Act created the Commission on Equal Employment Opportunity, which ensures the constitutional right to vote, and grants jurisdiction to the district courts of the United States to grant injunctive relief against discrimination in public accommodations. It also authorizes the attorney general to file lawsuits to protect constitutional rights in public facilities and public education.

Executive Order on Diversity, Equity, Inclusion, and Accessibility in the Federal Workforce
Executive Order on Diversity, Equity, Inclusion, and Accessibility in the Federal Workforce | The White House

In 2021, President Biden issued an executive order on Diversity, Equity, Inclusion, and Accessibility in the Federal Workforce. The order states that it was created to, "strengthen the Federal workforce by promoting diversity, equity, inclusion, and accessibility."

Per Whitehouse.gov, *"This order reaffirms support for, and builds upon, the procedures established by Executive Orders 13583, 13988, and 14020, the Presidential Memorandum on Promoting Diversity and Inclusion in the National Security Workforce, and the National Security Memorandum on Revitalizing America's Foreign Policy and National Security Workforce, Institutions, and Partnerships.*

This order establishes that diversity, equity, inclusion, and accessibility are priorities for my Administration and benefit the entire Federal Government and the Nation, and establishes additional procedures to advance these priorities across the Federal workforce."

TIP: *Visit the link below for an extensive list of diversity recruiting sources that can help you find the top diverse talent you need.*

https://codylhorton.com/thank-you/

LET'S CONTINUE THE CONVERSATION ...

As a wrap-up, I hope this book has provided you with ideas, options, and a framework for developing and implementing your diversity recruiting strategy. I have shared some highlights for best-in-class diversity and inclusion examples that will move you closer to creating inclusive messages and practices as you take the helm to establish values versus cultural fit inclusionary recruiting culture.

The goal of this book is to meet you where you are as a talent leader in the hope that you will build a flexible framework for internal and external relationships and engagement to connect with and build relationships with broader communities.

It is imperative to create an oversight committee or diversity steering committee to assign company-wide resources and goals. The example three-phase diversity strategy should serve as a roadmap of the kind of projects and initiatives that help your organization move forward with a plan. I tried to share a starter for how you measure progress between recruiting, sourcing and the practices associated with each player along the journey. I welcome the opportunity to help and look forward to support you as questions arise.

You can reach me at:

cody@codylhorton.com
Linkedin: https://www.linkedin.com/in/diversityrecruiter/

ABOUT THE AUTHOR

Cody Horton is the Founder and Managing Director for Diverse Recruiting Experts, which was acquired by HireBetter in late 2022.

"I was eighteen years old, about to graduate from high school. I felt really anxious and nervous about my future career opportunities as a young black man in a small Texas town.

"I was one of the first people in my family to graduate from high school, but I knew my family didn't have the money or the resources to help jump start my career with a job or sending me to college, so I enlisted in the Navy.

"Fortunately for me, my recruiter was intentional about recruiting diverse candidates for a program called the Boost Program to hire more women and people of color into the officer ranks of the Navy. I was selected for the program and earned a commission as a Naval Officer, ultimately achieving the rank of lieutenant commander. The experience changed my life and motivated me to be intentional about diversity over the past couple of decades.

"My teams have hired thousands of people into life-changing jobs at amazing companies and I believe that the Navy being intentional about diversity recruiting changed my life.

"When you're intentional about diversity and inclusion hiring, you empower people to change their lives and connect great people to great opportunities.

"Diversity has always been an integral part of my recruiting process, rather than something tacked on outside of it ... that's why the team at Diverse Recruiting Experts (now part of HireBetter) is so effective at finding great talent across a diverse spectrum of demographics.

"I love recruiting. It's so much more than finding someone to fill a vacancy ... it's an opportunity to change lives. Nothing is more satisfying than connecting individuals with organizations that offer an inclusive environment where their skills, talents, and unique perspectives will help them to thrive.

"My experience as a Naval Officer gave me the opportunity to gain leadership and management experience very early in my career, and I wouldn't trade it for anything. As a Naval Officer, I was given tremendous responsibility for people, operations, and assets. It was great to have the opportunity to solve management, technical, and people problems during my career in the Navy."

Cody earned a Master of Science in Management (Information Technology) from the Naval Postgraduate School, a Bachelor's degree from the University of New Mexico, and maintains his SPHR certification. Throughout his career, Cody has held several roles as Head of Talent Acquisition and Diversity Recruiting, where he was responsible for helping businesses attract and hire great people to build a diverse and inclusive workforce.

He embraces the use of technology in talent acquisition and has been a champion and thought leader for AI, Automation, and Video Interviewing technologies. As the Director of Campus and Diversity Recruiting for Walmart, Cody is instrumental in leading and innovating a shift towards virtual interviewing, innovative diversity recruiting efforts, and an enterprise approach to college recruiting.

Cody and his wife Dorothy live in Round Rock. They have two daughters who have graduated from college and are now empty nesters.

GLOSSARY

Diversity: The presence and recognition of individual differences among people, encompassing various dimensions such as race, ethnicity, gender, sexual orientation, age, socio-economic status, abilities, religious beliefs, and more.

Inclusion: The practice of creating an environment in which all individuals, regardless of their differences, feel valued, respected, and supported, and where they can fully participate and contribute to the organization's success.

Belonging: A sense of acceptance and connection within a community or organization, where individuals feel they can be their authentic selves without fear of judgment or exclusion.

Equity: The principle of ensuring fairness and impartiality in the allocation of resources, opportunities, and treatment, considering individual differences and needs. This may involve taking proactive steps to address historical and systemic imbalances or disadvantages faced by certain groups.

Equality: The state of treating everyone the same way, offering equal rights, opportunities, and resources, regardless of individual differences. While it promotes fairness, it does not always take into account the unique needs and circumstances of different individuals or groups.

Justice: The pursuit of fairness and impartiality in the distribution of opportunities, resources, and treatment, focusing on addressing systemic barriers and historical disadvantages faced by certain groups.

DEIB (Diversity, Equity, Inclusion, and Belonging): An acronym that encompasses the four interconnected principles and practices that organizations adopt to create diverse, inclusive, equitable, and supportive work environments.

Cultural Competence: The ability to interact effectively with individuals from diverse cultural backgrounds, understanding and respecting their values, beliefs, and practices.

Unconscious Bias: Unintentional, automatic preferences, or prejudices towards certain groups or individuals, based on stereotypes or personal experiences, that can influence decision-making and behavior.

Affinity Bias: The tendency to favor people who share similar backgrounds, experiences, or characteristics with oneself, often leading to preferential treatment during recruitment or promotion processes.

Microaggression: Subtle, unintentional actions or comments that convey negative or derogatory messages to individuals from marginalized groups, often reinforcing stereotypes and perpetuating discrimination.

Intersectionality: A concept that recognizes that individuals may identify with multiple overlapping social categories (e.g., race, gender, sexual orientation), which can lead to unique experiences of privilege or oppression.

Allyship: The active, ongoing process of supporting and advocating for marginalized groups by using one's privilege, resources, and influence to challenge and address systemic barriers and promote equity and inclusion.

Employee Resource Group (ERG): A voluntary, employee-led group within an organization that brings together individuals with shared characteristics, experiences, or interests to promote a diverse and inclusive workplace.

Talent Pipeline: A pool of potential candidates, both internal and external, who can be recruited to fill current and future job vacancies. A diverse talent pipeline ensures access to a wide range of skills, experiences, and perspectives, which can contribute to organizational success.

DOWNLOAD THE AUDIOBOOK FREE!

READ THIS FIRST

To say thanks for purchasing my book, I would like to
give you the Audiobook version 100% FREE!

I know you're more likely to finish this book if you have the audiobook.

Instead of paying $10-$20 for the audiobook,
I'd like to give it to you for free.

Download your copy here:
https://codylhorton.com/lp-audiobook/

Printed in Great Britain
by Amazon

26803180R00093